3 April 1997

Best Wishes

from

Peter Jackson

FIRST EDITION

Published by Vantage Press, Inc.
516 West 34th Street, New York, New York 10001

Manufactured in the United States of America
ISBN: 0-533-11422-5

Library of Congress Catalog Card No.: 95-90005

0 9 8 7 6 5 4 3 2 1

There are more things in heaven and earth than are dreamed of in your philosophy.

—William Shakespeare

BEYOND REASON

Prologue

Most of the old buildings are gone now, demolished, removed from the face of the earth for all time. Now is the time to write of the events that have happened to me and the stories and incidents relayed to me by people employed at Old Castle Works. The demolition will not change anything, except in the minds of those who read this. They are here; they are part of the territory; they are timeless and will still be here in a thousand years. They are harmless; any damage caused to people comes from their fear.

I have been at Old Castle Works since April 1984, and the incidents that have happened to me can only now be told to a wider audience. Speaking out before, to the disbelieving, would have damaged my reputation as a level-headed, well-educated engineer and technician. Now the current demolition programme is over, the stories become just stories and appear more acceptable to the people who still work at the factory. To report the incidents as they happened would have resulted in my being regarded as eccentric at best or a madman with a vivid imagination at worst. I did not want to damage my credibility, but now I can tell.

They? Who or what are they?

They are what have commonly been called ghosts or spirits or the walking dead. I do not think any of the descriptions suit all the events that have occurred. There is definitely a power of some sort at Old Castle Works, perhaps many powers; I do not know. I will relay the events to you and leave you to form your own conclusions.

Visitations from hell? Certainly not.

The walking dead? Maybe.

Guardian angels? Perhaps.

Unexplained power with intelligence? Definitely.

But let me begin at the beginning. . . .

Chapter 1

Old Castle Works was built over a period of time from the end of the nineteenth century almost to its demolition at the end of 1991. It was an old factory comprised of a number of buildings put together piecemeal and joined together to form a complex structure, with staircases and doorways that never seemed to have any sort of order or pattern. Anyone unfamiliar with the layout would soon become disorientated and lose his way. The site covers some six acres and is situated in the shadow of the ruins of an old Norman castle.

In A.D. 1090 the land was given to the Cluniac monks by Robert de Lacey to build a monastery on. Old Castle Works stood where a dam used to be, alongside the site of the monastery, and the events you are about to be told seemed to follow a pattern and were concentrated around the edge of the old dam.

The monastery was dissolved under the instructions of Henry VIII in 1539, and the buildings were dismantled during the 1550s. The factory car park was the burial ground for the monastery, and locals tell of excavation work taking place in the 1920s or 1930s that uncovered skeletons, many skeletons, so many that the local children would collect human skulls to use as candle holders at Halloween.

The place has a long history, too long to go into here. Anyone interested can visit the local museum, where all is recorded and on public display. I am more concerned with the immediate past rather than the distant past. There may be a connection, there may not, but certainly there is an energy source coming from this land. The monks may have been aware of it and built their monastery here because of it; who knows?

All Saints Church, dating back to the fourteenth century, is still in use today and was part of the overall scene of castle, monastery, and church. But enough of history.

I was appointed works engineer in April 1984. My duties included machine and building maintenance, services, health and safety, energy management, security, and anything else not directly concerned with production. My background was general engineering, even though I have a degree in mathematics and many other qualifications. My staff included electricians, fitters, joiners, painters, watchmen, cleaners, and general labourers.

From my unique position I was the focal point for complaints and reports of strange and unexplained events that the work force had come to take as part of their general working lives. Strange things happened so frequently that they were ignored until people began to lose patience; then they would complain. I was expected to explain events. Some, as you will see, were impossible to explain. When a pallet truck fully loaded with a half-ton load moves, unaided, for about twenty feet on a level floor or when water fills the factory without a leak or any source of the water whatsoever being found, how do you explain it to an anxious production director?

When I first arrived I called a meeting of my staff to introduce my techniques for dealing with breakdowns and fault analysis. As I was a mathematician, my method was logical progression through a sequence of events or functions to explain faults and so rectify or repair them.

One of my staff spoke up, telling me that my methods would not work here; at Old Castle Works things happened that defied logic and could not be explained by that method. My reply was, "Nonsense, I do not want to hear remarks like that; that is the easy way out. Thinking like that means you do not have to look for an explanation. You can just walk away and say it cannot be explained. That," I said, "is not my way of working." But within three months I was in agreement with him.

The stories can be put into two categories. First are stories that have been reported to me and I cannot verify as being factual. Second, are events I have witnessed myself, and these are absolutely true. It is not a case of whether the reader believes them or not; these things happened. They were, on occasions, witnessed by others at the same time as I witnessed them. Unfortunately, not believing such reports does not stop them from happening. If it did, my life would be a lot easier and my sanity more secure.

As I said earlier, the danger coming from these events is through fear. Fear alone is the enemy. I do not fear the power at Old Castle Works. I have lived with it now for many years, and I will continue to live with it. You cannot destroy a power such as this just by pulling down a building.

AND SO IT BEGINS . . .

I had been warned of the strange events that had become part of everyday life at the factory. *What nonsense,* I thought. *Why do they believe it?* This puzzled me as I went about my business as works engineer. Yes, there had been machine breakdowns that I found difficult

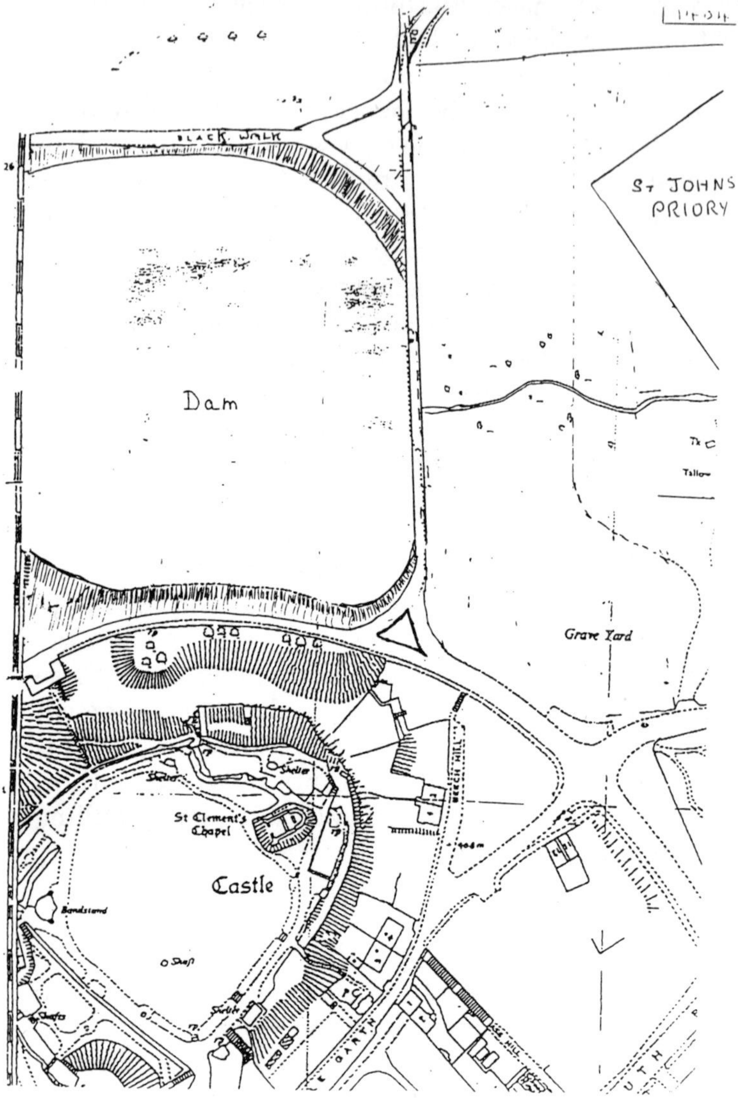

BLACK WALK
ST JOHNS
PRIORY
Dam
Grave Yard
Shelter
Shelter
St Clement's
Chapel
Castle
Bandstand
Shaft

1984

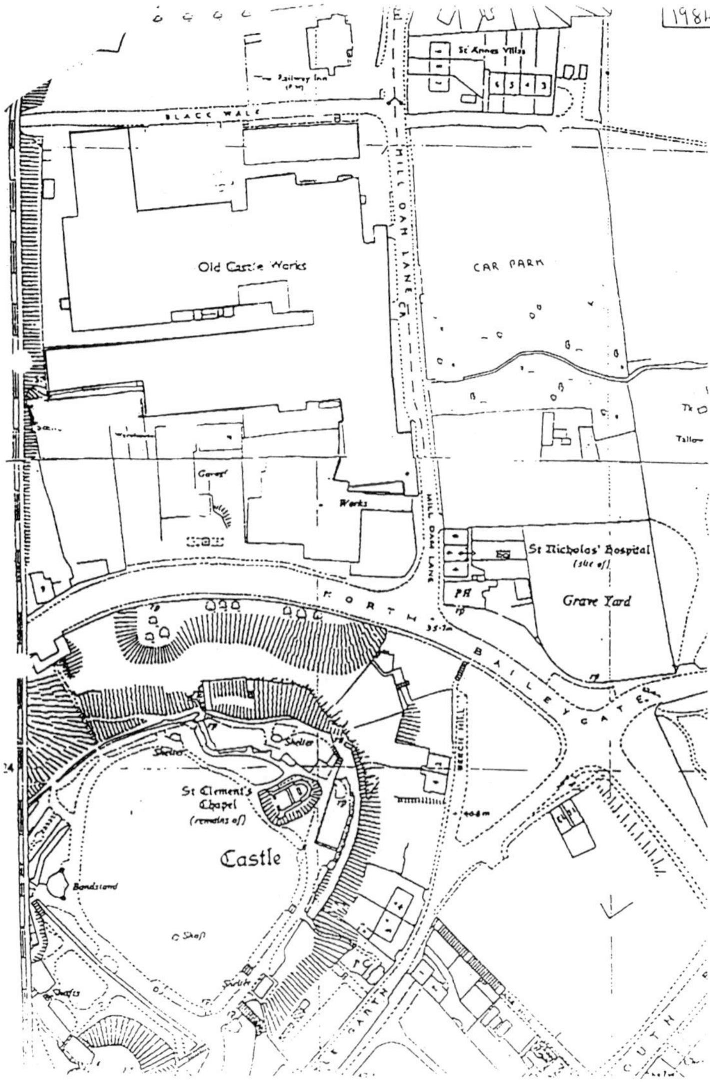
St Annes Villas
Railway Inn
BLACK WALK
MILL DAM LANE
Old Castle Works
CAR PARK
Works
MILL DAM LANE
St Nicholas' Hospital
(site of)
Grave Yard
PH
NORTH BAILEYGATE
Shelter
St Clement's
Chapel
(remains of)
Castle
Bandstand
Shaft
Shafts
GARTH
Tallow

to explain in logical terms, such as an electric motor suddenly starting to run backwards. This, as any engineer knows, cannot happen with a three-phase motor unless there is special control equipment, but it has occurred. The reason for it must exist; I just have not been able to find it yet. However, the number of unexplained events is increasing daily, and unless I can come up with some rational explanation, then I cannot prevent them from happening. This will mean I have failed as an engineer, and I'll be lucky to keep my job.

I was sitting at my desk, ploughing through a mass of paperwork that had accumulated, when the phone rang. It was the production director.

"Why did that machine break down and cost me a day's production?" he asked. "Someone said the motor started running backwards."

"Yes," I replied.

"How can that happen?" he asked.

"It must have been an internal fault in the motor, probably a short circuit in the wiring," I lied. "I have replaced the motor, and the machine is back in production."

"Good," he said, "but do all you can to see it does not happen again." With that he put down the phone.

There was nothing wrong with the motor. I had it checked by a specialist company. No fault had been found. This could not go on! How long could I keep coming up with believable excuses? The productions director only had to check with another engineer to find my explanations were, in the main, total rubbish. If this had been the only incident, it would not be too bad, but these unexplainable breakdowns were happening two or three times a week. Not only machine breakdowns either. Fire alarms had sounded and the factory had been evacuated, but there was no evidence of how or who triggered them. Even the fire chief was at a loss for an explanation. Toilets flushed with boiling water when the pipe work was connected directly to a large cold-water storage tank. Compressed air at 120 psi refused to travel down an open-ended steel pipe fitted without valves or pressure regulators. The pipe work was taken down to check for blockages, and daylight could be seen through the two-inch bore pipe. It was put back and tried again, but still the compressed air refused to travel down that pipe. The whole thing was getting out of hand. Was I losing my mind, or was there some explanation?

In desperation, I called a meeting of my staff: electricians, fitters, joiners, watchmen, and general labourers, ten people in all. When they were all assembled, I addressed the meeting.

"All right," I said, "what is going on? I know I have not been here very long, and it is usual to test out a new engineer, but things have gone too far. You have all been involved one way or another in these incidents, and I think it is a put-up job. Somehow, some or all of you know why these incidents are occurring. OK, you got me beat. I surrender. Why are they happening, and who is responsible?"

"Don't look at us," they replied. "We're the ones who have to do all the work. Do you think we like stopping machines from working? Fixing parts that don't have anything wrong with them? Why are you asking us?"

"Someone must know something," I said. "You've been here longer than I. Have things like this always occurred? How did the last engineer cope with it?"

"Yes, they have always happened," was the reply, "and the last engineer didn't cope. That is why you're here."

"OK," I said. "What is your explanation?"

"The place is haunted," they replied with one voice.

"Rubbish!" I exclaimed.

"Look, you asked for an explanation," one man replied. "Don't tell us 'Rubbish,' unless you can come up with a better one."

"Yes," I said in agreement. "I will listen to what you can tell me and try to keep an open mind."

"It's true," one of the watchmen spoke up. "I've been here a long time, and when I work nights things happen you wouldn't believe."

"Like what happened to the other watchman?" asked the electrician.

"What other watchman?" I enquired.

"There used to be three of us," said the watchman, "but one had a breakdown and was not replaced."

"What happened?" I asked.

"Are you sure you want to know?" he replied.

"Yes, I am sure."

"Well, sit back and listen, and I will tell you. Don't interrupt or comment until I have finished."

I agreed, and this is the story. . . .

It wasn't a cold and stormy night as the watchman made his rounds; it was a night like any other, as far as he was concerned. The factory was silent and dark. The upper floor was made of wood, and it would creak and groan as the temperature dropped. The watchman was used to the noises that occasionally broke the silence. He had been there for so long he didn't notice them anymore. He had made his base in the old reception office; this was no longer used as a reception area during the day, since the new office block had been built. The office was warm and provided a good view of the roadway outside; it had a telephone for emergencies and a toilet to the side.

Leading off from the old reception area was the first-aid room. A small room with a sliding door, it was always locked; only the watchmen and the nurse had keys. Inside the room was a bed to the left-hand side, situated with the top of the bed to the side of the doorway. There was a sink and a first-aid cupboard at the far end. A small oxygen cylinder for medical purposes was at the foot of the bed. The watchman never bothered to check this room; it was locked, and as there were no other entrances, no point in looking in there, he thought.

The watchman had completed his rounds. It was a little after 3:00 A.M. It would soon be daylight. He made himself a cup of tea. The electric kettle placed on the floor by the plug socket had just boiled. He began to read, yet again, yesterday's evening paper by the light of one sixty-watt bulb. Another boring night was nearly over.

Suddenly, an unfamiliar sound broke the silence. It seemed to fill the dimly lit room. He stood up quickly, his tea spilling over the floor. He stood still, quiet, his heart beating so hard that it almost jumped out of his chest. His ears strained to hear the sound again. Nothing, just the sound of his own heartbeat and his own breathing. Feeling rather foolish about himself, he began to clear up the spillage. Pulling a cloth from his overall pocket, he bent over to mop the floor. As he was bending down, a shadow passed across the other side of the first-aid room door. He saw it through the gap under the door, silhouetted by the outside lights shining in through the first-aid room window.

He realised someone was in the room. Straightening up and dropping the rag, he fumbled with the bunch of keys held by a chain from his belt. Taking hold of his torch, he unlocked the door and slid it to the side. He shone the torch quickly round the room. He was startled to see a figure on the bed, a figure wearing what he thought was a duffle coat with the hood pulled over its head. He nervously demanded to know what the person was doing there. No reaction came from the figure. He called again, but the figure still ignored him.

The watchman walked two paces into the room. He turned and shone the torch into the face of the figure. The hood was empty! The watchman's stomach sank as the empty hood slowly turned and looked straight at him. Shocked and terrified, he dropped the torch and ran out of the reception area into the blackness of the factory. Night-lights were situated at key positions, such as staircases and corners, but the factory was still very dark. He ran in a straight line down the factory as fast as he could.

Pain suddenly hit him in his right leg as he fell over some pallets or other obstruction. Dazed, he looked back towards the reception door; the light from the open doorway was cutting into the blackness. The figure was following. He could see it silhouetted against the doorway, following, following.

Panicking, he limped towards a staircase and struggled up the stairs to the upper floor. He desperately wanted to get out of the factory. The quickest way was by a fire exit, but they were locked. He fumbled to find the bunch of keys. They were gone. He must have broken the chain when he fell. What now? What should he do? Should he go back for them?

Looking back down the stairs soon made him decide. The figure was there at the foot of the stairs, the empty hood staring up at him.

He half-ran, half-limped, but mostly crawled his way along the upper floor towards a staircase at the far end. He needed somewhere to hide; his mind was racing.

At the top of the stairs was a ladies' toilet. He pushed open the door an went straight into one of the cubicles. Sitting down, he bolted the door and put his hands over his face. He was shaking, trembling with fright.

After a few minutes he began to calm down. Silence once again filled the empty factory. Slowly he began to remove his hands from his face. He blinked to try to make his eyes get used to the darkness. All he could see was the door in front of him. Suddenly, the figure came through the closed door, only twelve inches from his face. He passed out.

Just before 6:00 A.M. the work force began to arrive. The factory was still locked. Where was the watchman? He must be lying somewhere injured or worse. One of the managers arrived with a key. He immediately ordered an investigation.

A search was made and the watchman was eventually found in the ladies' toilet collapsed between the bowl and the wall. The door was bolted on the inside. One of the men climbed over from the adjoining cubicle to release the door and lift the watchman off the floor to allow the door to be opened.

An ambulance was called, and the watchman, in a state of severe shock, was taken to the hospital.

The watchman never returned to the factory, and even though he recovered, he swore he would never enter the building again. To my knowledge he never had.

My reaction to the story was a feeling of disbelief, but I said nothing. All the people at the meeting looked at each other in silence. Just then the phone rang. It was Dennis, the cabinet shop manager.

"Can you come to the flat panel department?" he said. "A woman has just collapsed."

I adjourned the meeting for an hour, while I investigated the problem in the cabinet shop.

When we reconvened, I gave my opinion of the watchman's story: "That was a very entertaining story, Jim," I said, "but one story does not mean the factory is haunted. In fact, I don't believe there is such a thing a 'haunted.' It's all in the mind of the person concerned."

"The breakdowns are not in the mind of anyone," said one of the men.

"That is the whole point of this meeting," I replied. "We have to find out why the machines are behaving the way they are. Is there any suspicion of the operators tampering with them?"

"The operators are woodworking machinists. They know very little of how the machines work," said one of the fitters, "but in some instances, that could possibly be the case. You can tell when that happens. They are simple problems, like someone changes a wire over or a pneumatic nylon tube. They are not major issues. The problems are when everything works as individual units, but the machine will not work as it should when the units are put back into position."

"Do you really think that the factory has some ghost or spirit wandering about with nothing better to do than play tricks on us?" I asked.

"When you put it like that, it does sound ridiculous," they replied.

"Of course, it's ridiculous," I said. "What puzzles me is why you are all so convinced that that is the cause."

"The stories and beliefs have been passed on from worker to apprentice for as long as anyone can remember," one of the men spoke up. "During and just after the

Second World War, anyone applying for a job was asked if he or she was afraid of ghosts."

"You're joking," I said, surprised. "You mean it was accepted as a fact, and they just came out and asked people before they were given a job? The applicant must have thought the management was a gang of lunatics."

"No, it was done much more subtly than that," said Jim. "It was a question that was on the application form. It was put there with a lot of other questions, which gave the impression that they were trying to form a profile of the applicant's personality, but it was put there so they knew that if they offered the person a job he would stay in that job and not give it up at the first unanswerable event that he witnessed."

"How long have these things been going on?" I asked.

"For as long as anyone can remember. It has always been accepted that the place is haunted. It's common knowledge, and everyone who works here does so in the full knowledge that strange things happen."

"I was never told," I said.

"I'm talking about local people, and besides, since the takeover in '78 the new management is probably unaware, not interested, or just does not believe it, like you."

"I must admit, I will take a lot of convincing," I replied, "but what you have said explains why everyone takes the events as normal. In the past, anyone who showed a fear of ghosts would not get a job; is that what you are saying?"

"No, quite the opposite. You only got a job if you did *not* believe in ghosts. Everyone was of the general opinion that they would lose their job if they showed any sign of believing in the hauntings. That meant no one ever reported anything. If anyone saw anything, he turned his back and denied everything. He carried on as though nothing unusual had happened. He would speak to other workers about it, but in those days they never told a boss. They would have been sacked if they had."

"That explains a lot. Do they still do that today?"

"No, but it has been inbred in a lot of the old hands not to make a fuss about such things. Just get on with the job, that's the general attitude."

"Where does that leave us?" I asked. "Back where we started, I suppose."

"No one has been able to explain what happens in this factory, but I can tell you that there are a lot of people out there who need to talk to someone. With you being new and in charge of health and safety, they are waiting to see how you measure up to the job. If you do, they will be wanting to tell you things and unburden themselves on you at the first opportunity."

"Thanks for the warning," I replied. "I don't mind listening, but whether I believe them or not is another matter. Right. Back to business. I am issuing a maintenance report form. Whenever there is a breakdown, I want the cause recorded. All those recorded as unknown I will investigate personally, and I will find the cause. I will put an end to this nonsense once and for all." With that I ended the meeting.

Put an end to the nonsense, that's what I'd said. If ever a mouth made a promise that the body could not keep, that must take first prize.

Chapter 2

Part of my duties was to look after the health and safety aspects of the running of the factory. This involved investigating accidents and near misses or any incident that affected the health, safety, and welfare of the employees at the factory.

Dennis, the cabinet shop manager, called me, in this capacity, to report that a female worker had collapsed screaming in the flat-panel department.

The nurse had been called, and she had asked for a stretcher to take the woman to the first-aid room. When I arrived I asked the manager what had happened.

He wasn't really sure; one of the lads had raced up to him to say Freda was having a fit. The manager had gone to her assistance but could not reach her because the way was restricted by loaded pallets. Someone was already with her, and the nurse had been called. He thought it important to clear a way through to her, so he ordered the loads to be moved. The nurse arrived with the stretcher, and Freda was carried to the first-aid room.

I asked to speak with the first man to reach Freda. During the interview I was told that he had heard someone shouting and screaming. He had stopped what he was doing and looked in that direction. He said that he had seen Freda in a severe state of distress and shouting, "Look out! It's going to get you!" or words to that effect. She seemed to be shouting to the man who was working in the spray booth.

I asked if he knew what she meant. He did not. He had not seen anything near Freda or near the guy in the spray booth, and by the time he had reached her she was lying on the floor, having hysterics. He could not make out what she was saying and had no idea what she had seen or what had caused her to act the way she did.

I then interviewed Bill, the man who had been working in the spray booth. Bill had no idea what had happened; he was working with his back towards Freda and with his ear defenders on, plus the noise of the booth, so he claimed he could not see or hear anything.

Later I spoke to the nurse, who said that she had taken Freda home, but Freda had refused to tell the nurse anything about what happened.

"Didn't you ask her?" I said.

Yes, she had asked, but Freda refused to talk about it and the nurse didn't want to force the issue.

Freda returned to work sometime later, but she would not speak of her experience to anyone and she refused to enter the flat-panel department again.

I interviewed Freda some two months or so after the event, and after much persuading and promises not to tell her workmates, I managed to get Freda to tell me what had happened. This is the first time I have told her story to anyone, and I hope she will forgive me for this betrayal of a confidence.

It was midmorning on a normal working day. The factory was humming with the noise of the machinery in the mill downstairs and the assembly shop was a hive of activity as Freda, one of the ladies who worked in the assembly area, was told by her supervisor to go into the flat-panel department and obtain some thinners. A small amount was all that was needed for cleaning purposes.

Freda took a small glass jar with her because the thinners were stored in five-litre cans. They were kept in a fireproof area away from where people were working. She entered the flat-panel department by the only doorway, a doorway some eight feet by ten feet, with a plastic strip curtain covering the opening. The air extraction equipment in use in the department always made the place feel cold. It was needed to prevent fumes building up within the workplace and thus reduce the fire risk.

Only four people worked in the flat-panel department, and one of those was employed spraying lacquer onto components via a spray booth. He always wore a face mask and ear defenders because of the nature of his work.

Freda approached him and tapped him on the shoulder to attract his attention. "Where do you keep the thinners?" she asked.

"Over there, lass," he replied in a broad Yorkshire accent as he pointed to a stack of cans in the corner.

"What? Right over there?" she exclaimed.

"Yes," he said. "Fire regulations, you see."

The tins were kept in a small area away from where the main work was carried out. The access to it had been blocked by pallets and work in progress.

Freda pushed her way through the stacks of panels and loaded pallets until she could reach the thinners. Placing her little glass jar on the floor after removing the top, she selected a tin of thinners that had already been opened. Carefully bending down to fill the jar from the tin, she sensed someone was directly behind her. She half-turned her head and saw movement out of the corner of her eye. She thought it was one of the lads trying to play a trick on her, so she continued with what she was doing. “I know you’re there,” she said. “If you make me spill this, I’ll brain you.”

No reply was forthcoming. Standing up, Freda put the top back on the can, placed the can back from where she had taken it, and turned round. What she saw made her blood freeze.

A figure some five feet tall was wearing a long brown cloak with a hood. The cloak was made out of rough blanket-type material; the hood was up and the head slightly bowed towards the floor. The sleeves of the cloak were longer than usual and hanging straight down the sides of the figure, but no hands were at the end of the sleeves. There was no face in the hood, and there were no feet sticking out from the bottom of the cloak.

Freda tried to scream, but no sound could she make. She tried to move, but her limbs would not work. All she could do was watch. The figure was some four feet away from her, and it stood there motionless for what seemed to be an eternity.

After a few seconds it turned to the right and moved away in a straight line towards the spray booth. The pallets of work blocking the way, which Freda had had to climb over, were completely ignored. The figure moved through the obstructions as if they were not there. The man working in the spray booth had his back towards Freda. He couldn’t see what was happening. The figure approached the booth. Freda could see what she thought was about to happen. She must warn him; she must.

Gathering all the energy in her body, she made a huge effort and suddenly found her voice.

“Bill!” she screamed. “Bill, watch out behind you!”

Bill couldn’t hear anything with his ear defenders and the noise of the booth.

The figure kept on going, nearer and nearer where Bill was working. Freda was beginning to get hysterical; she started screaming and shouting, all to no avail.

The figure floated straight on, past Bill, and disappeared into the back of the spray booth. Bill never noticed anything. The other men who were working in the department heard Freda shouting but couldn't get a clear view of her or the spray booth. Their line of vision was blocked by work in progress or machinery. They ran to Freda's assistance when it became obvious that she was in a state of distress.

"What's wrong, Freda?" one of the men called as he approached, quickly climbing over the obstructions.

"I thought it was going to get him! I thought it was going to get him!" she cried as she collapsed in a heap on the floor.

"Who? What? Get who?" asked the man.

Freda could not reply. She burst into tears and curled up on the floor.

"Get the nurse! Get the supervisor!" the man shouted to his mates. "I'll stay with her."

One man phoned down for the nurse while another ran for the supervisor. Bill continued working, oblivious to all that was happening around him.

The supervisor was the first to arrive. "Get these pallets out of the way!" he shouted at the men as he tried to reach Freda.

Men started running in all directions to move the obstructions and clear a pathway to Freda. The nurse arrived, took Freda, sobbing and trembling, downstairs, and attended to her. Later a car was ordered and Freda was taken home.

Is Freda's story true? It is easy to say it was her imagination, but an imagination so vivid as to put oneself into a state of shock is hard to believe. I am convinced Freda did see something, and like the watchman in the story before, she claimed she saw a hooded figure. The descriptions match and yet the two events were years apart. Freda did not know of any previous sightings, nor had she heard any previous descriptions.

There were many sightings of the hooded figure reported to me over the years. Most of the sightings were just fleeting glances, in or near the old reception area or the flat-panel department. No reports of hooded figures seen elsewhere in the factory were brought to my attention.

There are three more sightings worthy of telling. One is my own experience, which I will tell later, and one of the others involved a police officer.

*   *   *

There were two watchmen employed at the factory when I first started working there. They had many tales to tell, so many that it became difficult to decipher the truth from the yarns. They had many strange encounters, or so they claimed. None could be verified or disproved except one. These watchmen had no fear of the presence, nor did they make an issue of the facts. They simply learned to live with it. No harm ever came to them, and they continued with their employment until they retired in 1988. They would work twelve-hour days and twelve-hour nights on alternate weeks, with the exception of Saturday nights when the shift changed.

The night shift was a lonely time, and the hours would drag by with no one to talk to. The local policeman on his beat would call in to have a chat and a cup of tea. This would break the monotony, and it was reassuring to the watchman to know that if there were any problems or disturbances, the police were around to keep their eye on things.

The following story was verified to me by that policeman the day after, although what you are about to read will not appear in any police reports.

"Hello, Jim," said the policeman as he walked through the doorway. "My word, it's a cold night."

"Come in and have a drink of tea," replied Jim. "The kettle has just boiled."

Jim made the officer a cup of tea, and they both sat down to warm themselves by the one-bar electric fire.

"Much happening tonight?" asked Jim, trying to make conversation.

"No," replied the policeman, "just kids mainly, playing around with fireworks."

"Well, it is Bonfire Night next week, and you know what the kids are like around here."

"I certainly do," replied Jim. "I had to chase a gang of kids off the garage roof earlier. Cheeky little brats, you should have heard what they called me."

The conversation continued along these lines for about fifteen minutes or so.

"Better make a move," said Jim. "I've got to do my rounds."

"I'll come with you if you like," said the policeman.

"I'd like that," said Jim.

Off they went to walk the perimeter of the building. It was about 2:00 A.M. The night was cold and still. They crossed the road to check the lorry park. All the vehicles were secure. They proceeded down Black Walk, past the offices. A light from inside the offices cut into the night.

"Should that light be on?" asked the policeman.

"Yes," replied Jim. "It's left on for security. You can see if anyone is in there from here. It can't be switched off."

Continuing the patrol down Black Walk, they checked the timber yard gates and started back.

"Let's go into the factory the back way; it's warmer and we can check the interior of the building as we go."

"Good idea," said Jim, reaching for his keys. "It's better to vary the route."

They entered the building, which was in total darkness apart from the night-lights situated at key points around the building.

"Watch where you're going," warned Jim. "You'll need to use your torch."

Switching on their torches, they slowly made their way into the mill. From the bottom of the mill they could see all the way down to the old reception door at the far end. A night-light was positioned there because of the staircase running up to the right. Suddenly a figure appeared about ten yards from the old reception area. It was moving away from them, towards the door. The policeman saw it first. "Hey you!" he cried. "Stop!"

They were both about sixty yards from the figure.

"Stop, I say!" called the policeman again.

The figure kept on going slowly. It didn't turn or give any indication that it had heard them calling.

"He can't get out," said Jim. "That door's locked."

"No," agreed the policeman, "but if he gets up those stairs, we could lose him on the upper floor."

Jim and the officer both started running. Jim tried to keep up, but he was no match for the policeman, who raced after the figure as fast as he could. He ran down the mill, his eyes fixed on the figure in the dimly lit factory.

"Stop! I want to talk to you!" Jim cried.

The figure continued slowly towards the door. The policeman got within two yards of the figure. "Gotcha!" he cried, but the figure kept on going. It passed straight through the door and disappeared.

"Where did he go?" cried the policeman, his voice shaking.

"He was there and then he walked through the door; he literally walked through the door."

The policeman tried to open the door, but it was locked.

Jim hobbled up behind him. "What happened?"

"I don't know," replied the policeman. "He seemed to walk through the door."

"He did what?" asked Jim.

"I know what it sounds like," said the policeman, "but that's what happened. Open this door, quickly."

Jim fumbled for his keys for what seemed an age.

"Hurry up," said the policeman impatiently.

"Hang on, hang on," replied Jim.

Finally the officer found the keys and unlocked the door. They burst through the doorway only to find the room empty.

"There's no one here." said Jim. "Are you sure he didn't go up the stairs?"

"Look," said the policeman, his patience getting a little strained. "I was only six feet from him. I was about to put my hand on his shoulder, expecting him to stop, when he walked through the door." The policeman sat down. "Check the outside door, Jim. Did he get out that way?"

Jim checked the door. No, it was still locked.

"I don't believe it." The officer got up and tried the door himself. He thought for a moment. "I must have been seeing things; he's still in the building. I'll radio Base and get a car sent up. I want this building searched."

"Intruder at Old Castle Works," he called on his radio. "Send two officers to search the building. I have seen him myself, and I believe he's still in the building."

The radio crackled its almost inaudible reply: "Car and two officers will be with you in five minutes."

"Right. Jim," said the policeman. "I want all the lights on and all the doors to be kept locked, with the exception of the outside door."

Jim unlocked the door. "Shall I go and put the lights on?"

"No," replied the policeman. "We'll wait hear until the others arrive."

The car arrived about three minutes later, blue lights flashing but no siren. Two policemen got out of the car and walked into the reception area. "What's the problem?" they asked.

"There's a man in the building, about five foot two and wearing a long dark-coloured duffle coat with a hood. I almost had him, but he gave me the slip. Now one of you stay here and make sure no one leaves through this door; it's the only way in or out. Jim, if you'll come with us we can switch the lights on as we go."

Jim led the way. They searched the factory for about an hour and a half. No one was found, no sign of forced entry, and no indication at all that anyone had been on the premises. The two policemen from the car left at about 3:45 A.M.

"I don't like leaving you here, Jim," said the first policeman.

"Go on; I'll be all right. You've searched the place, and if there was anyone here, he's gone by now."

"Right," said the policeman, "but I'll be back at six to check if all is OK."

The policeman called back at 6:00 A.M., but Jim had nothing to report. All had been quiet for the rest of the night.

"What time does your boss arrive?" asked the policeman.

"He will be here about seven-thirty," replied Jim.

"I'm off duty at that time, but I'll be back to have a word with him."

I arrived and Jim was waiting for me. He told me the police had been down and would call to see me later that morning. Jim left at 8:00 A.M. the end of his shift.

The policeman arrived at about 8:45. I led him to an office where he relayed to me the events of the previous night. He told me that there would be an official report that an intruder had been sighted and a search made. He then asked if he could speak off the record. I told him he could, and he said that he had seen a figure, not six feet away from him, pass straight through a locked solid wooden door. He questioned my reaction. "You don't seem shocked or surprised," he said.

"No," I replied. "You are not the first to tell me of such happenings. There have been many such reports, and after working here I am no longer surprised at anything anyone tells me."

"That's a relief," he said. "I thought I was going insane."

"No," I replied, "but if you take my advice, you won't tell anyone outside this factory. They will never believe you."

*   *   *

It has been mentioned that there were no watchmen on duty on a Saturday night because of the changeover from the day shift to night shift. The local villains found out about this arrangement, and so most of the break-ins and vandalism would occur then. I found it necessary to engage the services of a security company to provide a guard for the nights when our own watchmen were unavailable. This next story is about one of those guards, who did not stay at the factory very long. His reasons for not wanting to stay alone at night come from the events you are about to be told.

The rain poured down as the security guard made his way down Black Walk. The night was dark and the wind lashed the rain against his face, making it difficult to see. His torch wasn't much use in the downpour. It just reflected the light back at him as it bounced off the raindrops, which came down so fast they formed a continuous sheet of water.

The railway bridge, which ran over Black Walk, would provide him with some shelter. The old bridge that carried the approach road to the station was a brick structure. The archway that formed the access for the public right-of-way beneath it was the only point of shelter between the main factory building and the timber yard.

Black Walk, as it was now called, stopped about fifty yards past the bridge and continued as a single footpath by the side of the timber yard fence.

The roadway was only used by the forklift truck and delivery drivers during the day and was full of potholes and puddles, which didn't help the security guard as he tried to find his way. He shone his torch on the ground, but with so much water about, it was difficult to tell the puddles from the solid ground. He was soaked. He could not risk running, as he might put his foot in a pothole and break an ankle, or worse. He cautiously made his way through the rain.

Black Walk has been a public right-of-way since medieval times, and in those days it was called Black Friars Walk. It was the route or approximate route the monks used as they made their way to the orchard.

The land to the right of the timber yard used to be the orchard and was full of apple, pear, plum, and cherry trees until the railway company decided to build the station and approach road at the end of the last century. The railway company built up the roadway by putting tons of earth to form an embankment, which cut straight across the site of the old dam. It also separated the six acres on which the factory stands. Now the only link between the two halves was under the old bridge.

The fruit trees, which were the descendants of the original orchard, were still bearing fruit until the late 1960s when they were all cut down.

All of this was of no interest to the security guard as he trudged his way through the pouring rain. He was only grateful that there was a bridge there to provide some shelter.

Finally he reached the bridge and leapt under it. He reached inside his coat for a cloth to dry his face.

He wondered if the job was worthwhile on a night such as this. He wiped his face and took off his cap, to shake the rain from it. He walked to the other side of the bridge and peered out into the rain. He couldn't see anything. It was pitch black and a mist was forming with all that water about. He shone his torch into the rain in the direction of the gates to the timber yard. The torch light made little difference at all. However, it did illuminate the underside of the archway.

He took the opportunity to have a quick smoke, switching off his torch and taking out his cigarettes and lighter.

The factory had a strict rule about smoking; it was not allowed in any part of the building. The only opportunity for the guard to smoke was outside the factory building—not easy on a night such as this.

Leaning with his back to the brickwork of the archway, he put a cigarette to his mouth and lit his lighter. It was from the light of the flame that he saw it.

A figure stood with its back to him at the other end of the archway. The figure was wearing a heavy hooded coat and just stood there, motionless, staring out into the rain.

The security guard apologised for not seeing him earlier and, switching his torch back on, tried to strike up a conversation. There was no reaction from the figure.

The guard did not seem to notice this; he just continued talking. Still the figure did not answer. The guard shone his torch away from the figure and down onto the floor. He did not want to embarrass whoever it was but still needed the archway to be illuminated. The guard started chatting away, as people who have to work alone always seem to do whenever they get the opportunity to speak to someone. They seem to cling to each visitor like a drowning man clinging to his rescuer.

All the time the guard was speaking, the figure did not respond in any way. It just stood there with its back to him, looking out into the rain.

This one-sided conversation lasted for about ten minutes, until the guard finished his cigarette.

The guard wondered why anyone should be stood under the bridge in the early hours of the morning in the pouring rain. However, it was a public right-of-way and he did not have the right to challenge the person or move him on. The guard had to check the timber yard but offered to help the figure find his way to the main road on his return.

Holding his coat together with one hand and pulling his cap down over his eyes, the guard walked out into the rain. Blackness once again filled the archway.

On reaching the timber yard gates, he checked the padlock. All was secure. The outside lights, high up on the timber yard wall, gave out a little light for him to see a little way into the yard. Everything was deserted.

The guard carried with him a small device clipped to his belt. This device was to show his control officer that he had done his rounds and at what time he was at a particular place. It worked by placing special keys in it and turning the keys. The keys were hung at specific points along his patrol route, and he would use them every time he passed each point. All the keys were different, and they were chained up so they could not be removed. There was one hung on the timber yard gates.

Undoing his raincoat to give access to the device, he dutifully placed the key in the slot and turned it. Once he had used the key he turned and quickly ran back to the archway. The roadway was in better condition on this side of the bridge.

As he entered the archway, he flashed his torch in the direction of where he had last seen the figure. He saw that it was still there. Walking towards it, he told whoever it was that he couldn't stay there all night and offered to show him the way to the main road. As he approached, the figure moved away into the rain. The guard called for him to wait for him. The figure did not respond. Out it went into the pouring rain, but not up the roadway; it headed off to the right, making an angle of about twenty degrees to the line of the roadway.

The guard cried out a warning. The figure was going in the wrong direction; he would walk into the fence.

The figure didn't stop or change direction. It disappeared into the continuous downpour of water.

The guard didn't follow immediately. He waited for the cry of pain or the sound of the figure hitting the fence. He heard nothing but the sound of the rain bouncing off the floor.

He followed shortly afterwards, moving as quickly as he could up Black Walk. He didn't see the figure again as he fought his way through the deluge back to the old reception area.

He stepped inside and removed his overcoat, shaking his hat to remove the water and stamping his feet. He hung his hat and coat behind the door and went into the toilet to find a towel. He needed to dry himself and also to use the toilet. With towel in one hand, wiping his face, he was standing in front of the bowl, relieving himself, when the lights went out.

Blackness filled the toilet.

A power cut. It would happen right at that very minute.

Standing very still, he finished what he was doing and slowly made his way out of the toilet. Feeling his way around the walls towards the door, he found it and fumbled his way towards the chair he knew was by the window. Sitting down, he peered out the window. Even the streetlights were out; he needed his torch.

He stood up and felt his way to the outside door, on which he had hung his coat. The torch was in the pocket. Finding the torch, he switched it on. Nothing happened.

The water had seeped in. Hitting the torch with his hand, he tried again. Still nothing.

Totally disillusioned, he found his way back to the chair. His eyes were now getting used to the darkness.

Sitting down, the towel still round his neck, he began to feel cold. He sat there cold, wet, and in the dark for what seemed ages. A strange feeling came over him; it started with a shiver down his spine. This feeling that he was not alone was overwhelming. He called out, demanding to know who was there.

His eyes peered into the blackness of the room, his ears straining for any sound. He could see and hear nothing.

He called again. There was no reply.

He thought it was his imagination, but the cold became more intense.

He sat there for another ten minutes, the feeling of another presence still with him.

He began to feel isolated, cut off from any help or assistance. He was cold, and wet, and feeling threatened; he decided to call Control. He could just see the telephone on a shelf at the side of the first-aid room door. He made his way towards it. Picking up the receiver, he dialled the number. The long, low *bleep bleep* of the engaged tone met his ear.

Frustrated, he was just about to put the receiver down when something gently stroked the back of his hand.

He cried out, startled. This was the last straw.

He stumbled and crawled finding his way to the outside door. Grabbing his coat and his hat, he ran out into the rain.

He put on his hat and coat when he was about ten metres from the building, and there he stayed, pacing up and down in the pouring rain, for over two hours. He was not about to go back into the building alone even when the power came back on.

As usual, the power came back on just after daylight, about half an hour before the next watchman arrived.

"What are you standing out here for?" the next watchman asked as he approached. "You're soaked."

"I'm not going back in there," his co-worker said. "They can stick their job. I waited here until you arrived—I was not about to desert my post—but I won't be back here again."

"What happened?"

"I'm off home. I'll see you in the pub tonight and tell you then, if you're interested. Oh, and by the way, there's been a power cut; all your clocks will be two hours slow." With that he was off.

The new watchman walked cautiously into the reception area. Everything looked normal. The towel was on the floor, the telephone off the hook, but apart from that, everything looked normal.

He walked into the main factory and looked at the clocks on the wall; they all showed the same time, the *correct* time.

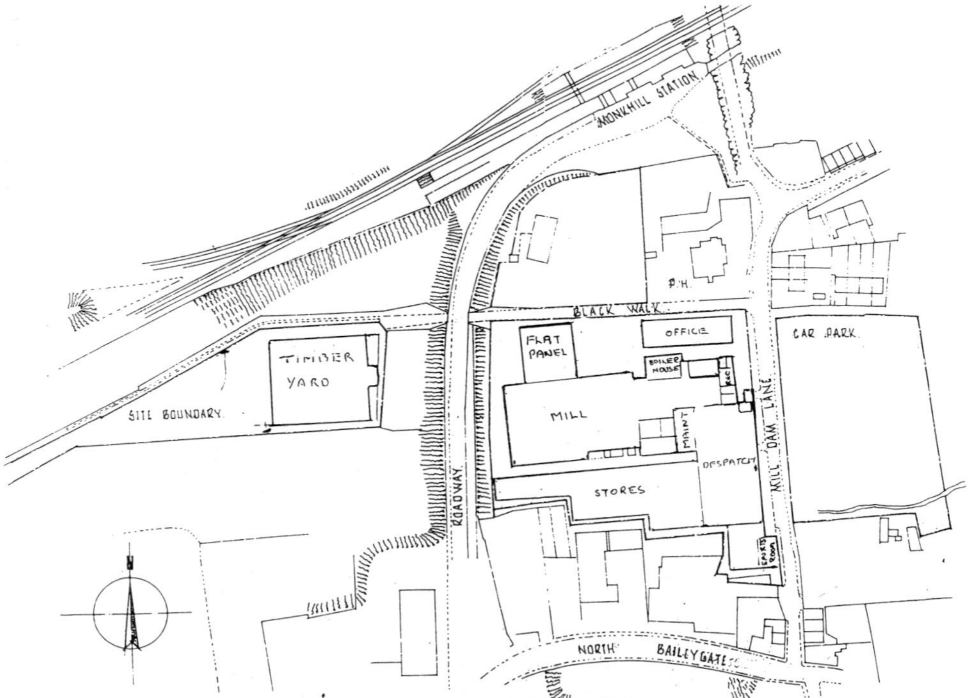

site location plan. 1984
OLD CASTLE WORKS

Chapter 3

Noises in an old building, particularly one with the upper floor made of wood, are very common. The wooden floor will creak and groan as the temperature rises and falls. The continuous movement of the wood meant the factory was never silent for long, but one sound that was familiar to us all and not accountable to the expansion and contraction of the woodwork was the sound of footsteps. Footsteps were heard so often that it was difficult to decide whether they were made by normal means or they were made by other means.

When the factory was empty and otherwise silent, footsteps could be heard quite plainly, from the ground floor, made by someone walking on the wooden upper floor. I have personally heard footsteps and, on occasions, dashed up the stairs to try to find the originator, only to find no one there so often that over the last few years I did not bother. I did, once or twice, find someone upstairs, but more often than not I found no one.

The following stories are cases of footsteps being heard when no one else was on the premises. These stories have been verified, in some cases by up to three people at the same time.

The polish shop, as it was called, was a department where the manufactured components were sprayed with lacquer. The lacquer used in those days was acrylic, which was highly flammable. The whole department needed to be flameproof—everything, the electricity supply, the fluorescent lights, and all the motors. The occasion arose when the electric wiring needed to be replaced, more lights were required, and in general the electric supply was in need of upgrading. The only way this could be done without closing the department was for the electricians to work after normal working hours, when the factory was empty.

This was arranged and the following story is an account of what happened while the job was being done.

Brian and Graham were busy working on the electric wiring. They were working some three metres apart, both working from stepladders, each with his own tools. Tools needed for the job were either placed on the top of the steps or kept in their overall pockets. Both men were becoming frustrated because their tools kept going missing.

"Have you had my pliers?" asked Graham.

"How could I have had them?" replied Brian. "I've been up this ladder all the time. I haven't been near you."

"I know that, but I've just used them and I put them on the top of the steps and now they're missing."

Both men stopped working and looked around without leaving their positions on the stepladders.

"They're over there," said Brian, pointing to a spot on the floor some four metres away.

"How did they get over there?" asked Graham. "I didn't hear them drop, and besides, they would have had to have been thrown to get over there."

Graham got down the ladder to retrieve his pliers. He climbed back up the ladder only to find the tools that he had left on the top of the ladder were gone. "What's happening here?" he exclaimed. "I left my tools up here, and now they're gone."

Brian, up the other ladder, started laughing.

"It's you, isn't it?" said Graham.

"No," replied Brian, "I haven't moved."

"What are you laughing at then?"

"The look on your face," said Brian.

"My tools keep moving on their own." said Graham.

"Don't be stupid," said Brian, still laughing.

"Where are my tools then?" asked Graham.

"They are over there," said Brian, pointing to the exact spot where the pliers had been. "You must have taken them with you and put them down when you picked up the pliers."

"I did not," said Graham, but to avoid arguments, Graham walked over, retrieved his tools, and continued working.

"I'm keeping my tools either in my pocket or in my hand from now on," explained Graham. He and Brian continued working in silence for about thirty minutes. Suddenly, the sound of footsteps broke the silence. The sounds were strange in as much as they suddenly started at a noise level that gave the indication that they were not too far away. They didn't start faintly and become louder as the person making them drew closer, but remained at a constant level, as though someone was marking time or walking on the spot. The footsteps had a strange ringing sound to them, like someone was walking on a metal staircase, although the nearest metal staircase was some distance away.

"What's that?" asked Brian.

"Must be the watchman." replied Graham.

"Never," replied Brian. "The watchman wears rubber-soled shoes, and besides, it's a wooden or concrete floor outside. That's the sound of hard-soled shoes on metal."

"You're right," said Graham. "We'd better investigate."

They got down their ladders, put their tools in their pockets, and went out of the department in the direction of the footsteps. Once they were outside the department, however, the noise seemed to be all around; it seemed to fill the entire area. The noise was not loud; it just seemed to fill the whole factory.

"Which way?" asked Graham.

"I don't know," replied Brian.

"Let's find the watchman; there's safety in numbers."

"Where would he be?" asked Brian.

"God knows," replied Graham. "Let's put a Tanoy out for him; that's the best way to find him."

The microphone for the public-address system was located in the old reception area. They both ran down the stairs, and Brian grabbed the microphone.

"Will the watchman report to the old reception area immediately please," the Tanoy boomed out.

Brian and Graham waited outside the door for what seemed an age. Meanwhile, CLUNK, CLUNK CLUNK, the footsteps continued.

"What's going on?" a voice behind them suddenly startled them.

"Christ Almighty, you nearly gave us a heart attack!" cried Graham. "Where were you, Jim?"

"I was in the toilet when the Tanoy bellowed out, and here I am. What's the problem?"

"Listen," said Brian.

"Listen to what?" asked Jim.

"Shut up a minute," said Graham. "Listen."

CLUNK, CLUNK, CLUNK, the foosteps continued.

"What? Those footsteps?" asked Jim.

"Yes," said the two electricians in harmony.

"Ignore them."

"What?" replied the electricians.

"Yes. I hear them often, never have found the cause. I hear them perhaps once a month They don't do any harm. People think you are daft if you tell them the next day, so ignore them; they'll stop in a minute."

"Well, I can't work under these conditions," said Brian. "I'm off."

"Don't be stupid," said Graham. "Think about it."

"What's there to think about?" asked Brian.

"Look. The job needs to be finished or the polish shop doesn't work tomorrow. People will be sent home, and when you are asked why you left the job, you will say you heard footsteps and ran home. Not only will you be laughed at; you will be lucky to keep your job. Besides, it's time and a half on nights."

"You're right," said Brian, "but I don't like it."

"I'll come and stand guard," said Jim, "but there is nothing to worry about."

The three men returned to the polish shop, and the electricians resumed working. The footsteps continued for a further fifteen minutes and then stopped as suddenly as they had started.

This story was reported to me by all three men the next day. I saw them separately, and each gave the same story. Either they had closely made up the story in great detail and conspired to fool me and the rest of the maintenance crew or they were telling the truth.

At this point, I had better explain about my staff. This will save confusion later.

First the watchmen. There were two of them, and unfortunately, they were both called Jim. There were also two people named Brian; one was an electrician, and the other was the maintenance supervisor. The second electrician was Graham, who has already been mentioned. Gary was the maintenance fitter.

As I said earlier, the two watchmen retired in 1988 and I lost contact with them. The electricians and fitters I still see on a daily basis, and they have expressed no objections to being mentioned by name. I am pleased about this, as it is my intention to be as factual as possible.

* * *

There have been many reports of footsteps, as I have stated. Graham first heard them when he was a young apprentice, back in the late seventies. He was working with a qualified electrician after normal working hours. Graham was left alone for a couple of minutes while his mate went to another part of the factory. When Graham heard footsteps on the floor above, he thought it was his mate. When the electrician returned, Graham asked why he had been upstairs.

"I haven't," replied the mate. Graham did not believe him, as they were the only two people in the factory at the time. The electrician insisted that he had not been upstairs, but Graham did not believe him. Graham thought that he had been told this just to be teased and made to look a fool. He remembered the event, however, and was reminded of it when heard the footsteps again while working in the polish shop.

On another occasion, Brian and Gary were working in the flat-panel department, repairing a machine. It was a shutdown period, and only the maintenance crew was working.

Brian was on his back under a machine when he realised a special spanner was needed in order to complete the work. He asked Gary to go back to the workshop for it. Off Gary went. The workshop was some distance away and Brian knew it would take Gary a good five minutes to walk there, find the spanner, and walk back. Brian continued working under the machine.

He's taking his time, Brian thought after five minutes had passed. Then he heard footsteps. *He's here at last.*

The footsteps came closer and closer and stopped alongside where Brian was working. He stuck his hand out from under the machine, expecting Gary to place the spanner in his hand. Nothing happened.

"Come on," said Brian. "Pass me the spanner."

Still nothing.

"What are you playing at? Give me the spanner."

Still no response. Losing his patience, Brian climbed out from under the machine. The department was empty. There was no one there at all.

A few minutes later, Gary arrived. Brian told Gary what had happened.

"You must have been hearing things," said Gary.

"Yes, you are probably right," replied Brian, and they carried on with the job.

Footsteps are something that cannot always be put down to hauntings. There are so many explanations: an intruder on the premises, an employee working late, even water dripping on a metal sink being mistaken for footsteps. However, the footstep reports were so frequent and unexplainable that I, as well as everyone else, took Jim the watchman's advice and ignored them. Footprints, however, are more difficult to ignore.

The factory was a woodworking factory, and dust from the machines was a constant problem. Dust extraction equipment of the highest standard was in use, and the factory was kept very clean, as factories go, with general daily cleaning and an annual vacuuming of overhead lights, pipe work, and beams, but when the factory was shut down for the annual holiday period, a light film of dust settled over everything. In the cabinet shop, where the furniture was built, the wooden floor had worn particularly smooth and the constant use of wax on the finished furniture had, over the years, given the floor a smooth, shiny finish, so much so that certain areas had to be painted with antislip paint for safety reasons.

On this occasion, it was the first day back after the summer shutdown and, as usual, everything was covered by a light film of dust. Alan was the first to be at his bench. He was a cabinet maker, and his workbench was in the centre of the department. On the way to his bench he noticed footprints in the dust on the floor. The footprints caught his attention because they were smaller than the average foot. They were also from plain-soled shoes, not safety shoes with a heavy tread pattern as normally worn on the slippery floor. More of a sandal-type footprint, he thought. He followed the footprints, thinking kids had broken into the factory to steal his tools. He followed the footprints in the direction of his bench and, to his amazement, the footprints went over the furniture that had been built before the holidays. The footprints led up to the production conveyor, on which was placed a row of storage units. The units stood some 1.6 metres high, and the footprints went straight over the top of them. The dust on the top was undisturbed apart from the footprints; also, the distance between the footprints was the same as the distance between those on the floor. It was as though someone had walked over the storage units as if they were not there. This made Alan start laughing and call his fellow workers over. Intrigued, the small group decided to follow the footprints. The prints went over every obstacle in their path, but the spacing of the prints never changed. Suddenly they came to an abrupt halt in the middle of an open space, not near any walls or benches or near a low roof. The footprints just stopped, with no evidence of the person responsible leaving the spot. This caused great interest and more people joined the group, and as you would expect, the evidence was soon destroyed. Was this a hoax or maybe someone playing a joke? Who knows? Just another mystery of the old factory.

Chapter 4

I will now begin *my* story. I had listened to many tales of supernatural events from the people who worked at the factory. I had listened quietly and patiently, mainly because the people who had experienced them needed to tell their experiences to someone who would not laugh at them or ridicule them. Personally, I did not believe a word of it, but doubts were beginning to creep into my mind and the machine breakdowns were continuing to happen. . . .

A transport lift that operated between floors to bring the finished goods from the assembly area to the transport department was a particular piece of vital equipment. When it broke down there was no other way to get the goods into the vehicles for dispatch. The normal way it was operated was for it to be loaded on the upper floor and unloaded on the ground floor. It was then returned empty to the upper floor. It was a transport lift for goods only, and people were not allowed to travel on it at all. This rule was rigorously enforced.

The lift was a screw-jack type of lift, which consisted of a metal platform with four long threaded rods, one at each corner. The controls for the lift were situated at both ground and upper levels on the outside of the lift doors. The lift was driven by an electric motor through a reduction gearbox. This drove a chain that went all the way around the platform and in turn drove four threaded sprockets. These moved the lift up and down the threaded rods when the motor was activated.

The safety devices were quite extensive. They consisted of three electrical switches that were operated by the lift platform itself. The first switch stopped the motor driving the lift when it reached the correct position. The second allowed the door to be opened and cut the electric supply to the motor so the lift could not be operated with the doors open. The third was an emergency switch that cut all electricity supplies if the other two switches failed. When this happened the lift could not be operated at all until the maintenance team had checked the operation and the electrical supply had been restored.

On this particular day the lift was being sent back to the upper floor when it stopped, changed direction, and crashed into the bottom of the lift shaft. It had gone past the ground floor position, ignoring not one but three electrical switches, any one of which should have stopped the lift from reaching the bottom of the shaft. The motor had continued running and had driven the platform into the pit below floor level with such force that it had driven the threaded rods, which were over twelve feet long, out of their mountings and bent and buckled them all.

I immediately put the fitters to work on repairing the lift and asked the electricians to provide me with a full fault analysis of the electrical circuit and a full report of why it had failed. Luckily, we carried a full set of spares for the lift mechanism, and I asked the maintenance crew to work as late as necessary to have the lift back in full working order by the next morning.

A short time later the electricians reported back that there was no fault with the electrical circuit and, what is more, no damage to the three limit switches, which were still in working order.

This I did not believe; I needed to see for myself. To my amazement, the switches were there in their correct position with the lift platform below them. This could not have happened, particularly with switch number three. This switch was situated in the direct path of the platform. For this switch to still be intact, without a mark on it, it would have had to pass through a half-inch steel plate, but there it was, a large, heavy steel platform below a small electrical switch that was fastened to a thin steel bracket. The switch was still covered with dust and dirt, with no evidence at all of anyone removing or replacing the switch. I looked on in amazement, but you have to be positive in these situations, and I instructed the fitters and electricians to carry on and get the lift operational by the next morning. I said I would call in later that evening to see how the job was going and to sort any problems that they might have encountered.

On my way home I puzzled over how the lift platform could have got below the switches without disturbing them. The thought that the factory was haunted kept coming back into my mind.

Before I started work at the factory I was convinced that hauntings, ghosts, and the like were just figments of the imagination. Their place was in books or films, not part of real life at all, but the evidence was becoming overwhelming.

Other people's reports of sightings and hearing noises I found quite entertaining. When I was told them, I tried to be sympathetic and listen. When someone tells you, face to face, you can look into his eyes as he speaks. They told me their accounts of what happened with such sincerity and conviction that I believed that they believed them.

The machine breakdowns and other happenings were mysterious, and I could not explain any of them, but surely that was a failing on my part, a lacking in my own ability, not ghosts or other such nonsense. Now I have seen electrical switches mounted directly in the path of a large metal platform, switches that should have been smashed to pieces with the impact or bent out of position, still intact and in full working order but with the platform below them. What are the possible explanations? I began to list them in my mind. Someone could have removed the switches and deliberately run the lift platform into the ground, smashing the lead screws, breaking the chain. He then could have gone into the lift shaft and repositioned the switches.

No, this explanation seemed too farfetched. How did he gain access to the shaft? The doors only opened when the platform was in the correct position.

He could have climbed into the lift, stood in the maintenance alcove while the lift went past, jumped into the pit, removed the switches, got back into the alcove, waited until the lift came back down, knowing that it would crash, jumped back onto the platform, replaced the switches, and . . . How did he get out?

I dismissed this explanation for several reasons:

1 The switches were covered in dust and dirt, with no sign whatever of having been replaced.
2 In order for the switches to be removed, they would have had to be disconnected and this would have stopped the lift from moving.
3 If anyone had been in the lift shaft when the platform crashed, he would have been killed, with all the bent and twisted metal flying about.

4 When the lift crashed it created a lot of attention and people immediately looked through the observation windows in the lift doors at both levels. They would have seen anyone replacing and reconnecting three switches and would have somehow had to release the door to let the person out.

I tried to think of another possibility.

Someone had removed the platform and replaced it under the switches? Rubbish, the platform weighted over two tons, the lead screws passed through the platform, and the lift shaft was only six inches wider that the platform in both directions. I dismissed this explanation immediately. There was also the question of why anyone should want to do this. Just to fool me? No, there were a lot simpler ways of doing that. I was just running out of possible explanations.

At around 8:00 P.M. I returned to the factory. The production director was waiting for me.

"Come to my office," he said.

I walked behind him into the office.

"Will the lift be repaired by morning?" he asked.

"I will make sure it is," I replied. "We have all the spares and we will work through the night to make sure it is in full working order."

"Right," he said. "But why did it happen? The electricians say it wasn't an electrical fault; the fitters say it wasn't a mechanical fault. Well, what was the fault?"

"You've been talking to the men, I see."

"Of course I've been talking to the men. I haven't been home yet. Why did it happen?" he repeated.

"I don't know," I replied.

"YOU DON'T KNOW! YOU DON'T KNOW!" he shouted, banging the desk with his fist. "Don't ever, ever tell me you don't know. I pay you to know. I don't want an engineer who doesn't know. Now get out there and find out. I want a full explanation. By 9:30 tomorrow morning be in my office with some answers."

With that I left. I couldn't blame him; I would have reacted in exactly the same way in his position.

I went to the lift shaft where the crew were working.

"How are things going?" I asked.

"OK," said Brian. "If he hadn't been here we would have got on a lot better."

"Who?" I asked.

"That director. He's been looking over our shoulder, asking questions. If he wants the job finished, he should shove off and let us get on with it."

"Yes, I know, he's just had me in the office; he wants an explanation of why it happened by tomorrow morning."

"Best of luck," said Brian.

"Have you found any reason for it?"

"Sorry," he replied, "but I've been more concerned with putting it right than looking for a cause. The electricians may have an answer."

"Don't ask us." They had overheard and one answered, "We've checked and double-checked the wiring, the switches, contacts, relays, cutouts, and main supply. Everything is working as it should."

"What about those switches?" I asked.

"Yes, what about those switches?" he replied. "I've no idea why they weren't broken beyond repair. Mind you, it's a good thing they weren't; we don't have any spares of those."

"Have you got everything you need to complete the job?"

"We don't need anything; we're not replacing anything. We'll just check the circuits and reposition the switches when the fitters have finished."

"Good," I said. "All I have to do now is find an explanation for it happening by tomorrow morning."

"Tell him a relay welded itself together. He'll never know; he wouldn't know a relay from a tin of peas," said Graham.

"But what about the switches still being in position?"

"He doesn't know about that; we haven't told him. Have you?"

"No."

"Well, don't tell him. He wouldn't believe you anyway."

"You're right about that," I replied. "Well, what I tell him is my problem. Thanks for working over to get the thing fixed."

"No problem," they replied.

"I'll get the coffees," I said. "Everyone want a coffee?"

"Yes," they replied.

"OK, five coffees coming up."

With that I walked away from the lift shaft for about twenty yards. I turned right through a sliding door. The coffee machine was about thirty yards away at the bottom of a flight of stairs. I reached the machine, put the money in, and dialled for three coffees white with, one coffee white without, and one tea white with. The drinks came in plastic cups. Trying to carry five hot drinks in plastic cups isn't easy, so I found a flat piece of board to use as a tray.

I walked back very carefully, trying not to spill the coffee. When I reached the sliding door I had difficulty.

It was a large, heavy door eight feet high by six feet wide, weighted so it would close itself after it had been opened. It was a large fire door and must always be kept closed. In order to get through the door I had to put the tray on the floor, open the door, hold it with my left foot, bend down, pick up the tray, and quickly walk through the door before it closed behind me. Having negotiated the door successfully, I walked carefully back to the lift shaft, both hands holding the tray.

Something touched my face, something very gentle and light. It tickled, like walking through cobwebs. That was just what I thought it was. I shook my head and continued walking.

It happened again, heavier this time, almost like walking through a lace curtain. Again I shook my head, but this time I stopped and looked around me. There was nothing near me. No cobwebs, no curtains, nothing.

"Here comes the coffee," I heard someone say. It was one of the fitters. This attracted my attention back to what I was doing.

The lads had stopped work when seeing me approach and were standing around waiting for their coffee. I had taken two or three more paces towards them when suddenly something covered my face completely. It was as though someone had thrown a sheet or tablecloth over my head. I panicked. I couldn't see where I was going, and I couldn't understand what it was.

The tray of coffee went up in the air as I put both hands to my face to try to pull whatever it was off. My hands reached my face, and my vision was restored in time to see five cups of coffee and the tray landing on my chest.

This proved a great source of amusement to the maintenance crew, who had seen it happen.

"Is that the latest dance?" one man said as I danced around, the hot coffee running down the front of my trousers.

"Do it again; I missed it," laughed another.

"Something covered my face," I said. "I couldn't see."

"Sure it did," the first man said. "You just tripped; stop making excuses."

The laughter continued along with all the relevant witty comments.

"I'm going to get cleaned up. You can fetch your own coffee in the future." With that I went to the washroom to clean up.

My shirt, my trousers, and my pants were soaked. It had even run down my legs into my shoes. I cleaned myself up as best I could and went back to the men.

Still smiling, the men had resumed work, and the job was almost complete.

"Right. I'm off home. I will see you in the morning." With that I walked out of the factory.

Someone shouted, "Aren't you having a coffee before you go?"

Hearty laughter broke out again, and I left them to get on with the job.

I didn't sleep very much that night, my mind going over the events of the previous day. I was beginning to feel very depressed. I couldn't explain the events that had led to the machine breakdown or the fire alarms sounding or all the other happenings. I was having to lie to my directors, and now I was a laughingstock in front of the men. I was feeling about as low as you can get. I was beginning to feel a total failure.

I arrived back at the factory at about seven-twenty the following morning. The watchman was standing there waiting for me. This was always a bad sign, as he only wanted me when there was a problem.

"What's up, Jim?" I asked. "Didn't they finish the lift?"

"Oh, yes, the lift is fixed; the lads didn't leave until 3:00 A.M. That's the problem. They won't be in until ten o'clock, and I can't get the compressor to start."

Not another thing, I thought. *How much can I take?*

The compressor was a vital piece of equipment. Without it the machines could not work.

"What about the standby compressor?" I asked.

"Tried it," said Jim. "That won't work either."

Oh, no, no compressors, no maintenance crew until 10:00 A.M. This was the end of the line. I would be sacked as soon as the production director arrived.

"Right, Jim," I said. "I'll have a look myself."

"Hope you get it running," said Jim. "The mill lads are standing by their machines waiting to start work."

I went to the electricians' workshop, picked up the Avo meter, and went to the compressor house. I checked the electric supply, the switches, the relays, the cutouts, the control circuits, the pressure switches, everything I could think of. Everything was working as it should. I even checked the motor to see if it had burnt out, but no, it was fine. Still the compressor refused to start.

In a mixture of anger, frustration, and sheer desperation, I stood up, clenched my fists, put my head back, and shouted, "WHY ARE YOU DOING THIS TO ME? WHY CAN'T YOU LEAVE THINGS ALONE? OK, YOU ARE THERE! YOU HAVE CONVINCED ME YOU ARE THERE! NOW LEAVE THINGS ALONE! I CAN'T TAKE ANY MORE!"

Tears running down my face, I closed my eyes and stood still for a few seconds. Pulling myself together, I pressed the start button again. The machine burst into life. I was astonished. I couldn't believe it, but the machine was running.

I put the covers back on the machine and collected my tools together.

As I was leaving I stopped, looked up, and said, "Thank you." Then I left.

I went to check the lift. All was well; everything seemed to be working normally.

At 9:30 A.M. I reported to the director's office as he had asked.

"Come in," he said. "Is the lift working?"

"It is," I replied.

"Did you find the cause?" he asked.

"Yes, it was . . ."

"That's all right," he cut me off. "As long as *you* know the cause, that's what counts. I don't need to know. Good work."

"Thanks," I said and left.

I had been let off the hook. I didn't need to make an excuse. He didn't want to know what had caused it after all; he just wanted to make sure I knew. I didn't, but that didn't seem to matter anymore.

Chapter 5

Things seemed to improve after the events in the compressor house. The machine breakdowns on the whole were normal. The incidents where the breakdowns did not have a rational explanation were becoming less and less.

As time went by and the memory began to fade, I again became very sceptical about the idea that the place was haunted. *Coincidence!* I thought. I had however, formulated a little ritual that I did every morning. When I arrived each morning, as I walked into the factory, I would say, "Good morning, Charlie. Let's have a peaceful, uneventful day. I know you are there; you don't have to prove anything." Why I did this I really don't know. I didn't see it did any harm; it was a form of insurance, I suppose. I would never let anyone hear me, of course, and I didn't really believe it myself anyway.

Why Charlie? I often thought to myself. *How did I come to choose that name?* I didn't know and I still don't know. It just came into my head.

I made it known among the maintenance crew that I had nicknamed the ghost, their ghost, Charlie and this is how it is still referred to today. It became easier to say, "Charlie's been at it again," and we all knew what was meant. It saved trying to explain to anyone who overheard us talking about unexplainable events. Anyone today could ask any of the maintenance crew about Charlie and he would know exactly what you were asking about. Calling it Charlie also somehow made it feel more acceptable, easier to live with, not a thing to be feared, more a mischievous companion than an enemy.

The mysterious breakdowns had not ceased altogether, but no major incidents had occurred that defied explanation. There were many smaller incidents that happened, and when they did, the fitters and electricians would come to me and say, "Come and have a look at this machine. I've tried everything and I can't get the thing to work." As I walked to the location of the machine, I would say to myself, *Come on, Charlie; leave things alone,* and when I arrived I would say to the operator, "Give it a try," and the machine would start immediately. I know this sounds unbelievable, but it happened many, many times and was witnessed by dozens of people. It seemed that I didn't have to do anything; I just had to be there.

On one occasion I can remember, I had to visit another factory. I did not arrive back until about 3:00 P.M. It was a cold January day. When I arrived back at the factory it was freezing. Everyone was wearing scarves and coats. Hot soup had been provided by the management to try to keep the work force warm and working.

When I arrived in my office, the phone rang; it was the factory manager.

"Thank goodness you're back." he said. "I saw you arrive. Can you see what you can do to get the heating on?"

"Why? What's wrong?" I asked.

"The boiler's broken down and the maintenance lads have been working on it since seven-thirty this morning without a break."

"Right." I replied. "I'll go to the boiler house now and see what the problem is."

I went to the boiler house and I saw the two fitters working on the top of the boiler. It normally produced steam at 150 degrees Celsius and ran at four bar pressure. The steam was fed through steel pipe work to heat exchanges in the factory.

I walked round to the front of the boiler and looked at the pressure gauge. The pressure was up to four bar. I walked over to the pipe work manifold; this was the distributions point for the steam. It consisted of a large pressure tank from which pipes of various diameters ran each with a control valve to control the amount of steam that went to each section of the factory. The manifold was cold.

"What's the problem, Brian?" I shouted to the leading fitter.

"Oh, you're back," he replied. "Thank God for that. Hang on; I'll come down." He climbed down the ladder from the top of the boiler.

"What's wrong, Brian?" I asked. "The pressure's up, but the pipe work is cold."

"I know that," he replied angrily. "I've been working on it since this morning. I've had no lunch yet. For some reason the steam won't go down the pipe."

"Is the valve open?"

"Of course it is," he said impatiently.

"It must be waterlogged with condensate."

"No, I've drained the manifold."

"What else could it be?" I asked.

"You tell me," he said.

Suddenly the manifold started to bang and shake.

"What the . . ." said Brian. "The steam's going through now; that banging is the thermal shock as the hot steam hits the cold pipes."

"Well, that's alright then," I said. "Go and get some lunch, and I will see you in my office when you've finished."

I returned to my office. Ten minutes later the phone rang; it was the works manager.

"I don't know what you did," he said, "but keep doing it."

"I didn't do anything," I replied.

"Stop being modest," he said. "The lads have been working on it for over seven hours with no results; you walk in and ten minutes later we have heat. Thanks for whatever you did." With that he rang off.

Half an hour later, Brian came in. I could see by his face he was angry.

"Sit down, Brian," I said. "What's wrong?"

He didn't reply. I didn't press him. I could see he was choosing his words very carefully. I sat and waited.

Finally he spoke. "You made us look like pillocks," he said.

"Why do you say that," I asked.

"We'd been working on that boiler since we arrived this morning, no results. You walk in and ten minutes later it's working. Everyone thinks you did it."

"I didn't do anything."

"I know that, and you know that, but everyone else thinks we need you to hold our hands all the time."

"I'll tell them the truth."

"They won't believe you; they will think you are trying to protect us."

"I can't help what they believe; would you rather the boiler not be working?"

"No," he replied. "I just wish you hadn't come back when you did."

"You were glad to see me when I walked in."

"I didn't know the steam was going to go through ten minutes later."

"Well, I'm sorry, but I will make sure you get the credit for fixing the boiler."

"I don't want the credit; I just don't want the blame for it taking all day to fix it."

"No one's blaming you."

"OK," he said, calming down, "you must have the Devil on your side; that's all I can say."

His words stuck in my mind. I've got the Devil on my side, have I? That's what he said. I've got something on my side at last, but not the Devil, definitely not the Devil.

The incident with the heating did my reputation no harm at all, as you can imagine, but Charlie had not finished with me yet. Not by a long chalk.

* * *

The breakdowns of a mechanical and electrical nature I seemed to have under control. The sightings had for the most part ceased. It was as though Charlie had become bored with this and wanted to try a few new tricks.

By the side of the factory entrance, between the boiler house and the old reception area, was a suite of offices. They were used, at that time, as the drawing and design office. Adequately furnished, they had suspended ceilings and a wooden floor. The walls were studded out with plasterboard and wallpapered. The lighting was good, as it would have to be for the area to be used as a drawing office.

On this particular day, everything was running normally. All the machines were working, goods were being produced, and everything was running smoothly for once.

As I was walking past the drawing office, there was a commotion as three draughtsmen came running out holding handkerchiefs up to their faces, covering their noses and mouths.

"What's going on?" I asked.

"Just go in there and see for yourself," one man said.

I walked into the office, and it hit me: the most awful smell that I had ever smelt in my life. It was disgusting, and the strength of it was overpowering. I ran from the room. The stench was making me ill.

"Good grief," I said when I had recovered. "How long has that been there?"

"It came just a few seconds ago."

"It must be a dead rat under the floor," I said.

"Ten dead rats is more like it!" they cried.

"Stay out here for a few minutes; see if it clears." With that I went to find the joiner and his mate.

The smell was really bad—rotting meat or something like it, but many times more powerful than anything I had ever smelt before. I returned with the joiner and went with him into the room, holding my handkerchief to my face. The smell was just as bad as before. We could not stand to be in the room for more that a few seconds. We ran out again.

"What do you think of that?" I said.

"That's awful," he said, "but what do you want me to do about it?"

"It must be a dead rat or something. You'll have to take the floorboards up and find it."

"I can't work in that stink," he said.

"No," I replied. "Get a car and go out and fetch two face masks. Tell the supplier what they are for and he will supply the correct ones for the job."

"Right," he said, and off he went.

I went to see the drawing office manager. I entered the office from the other end to try to avoid the stench. People at that end of the office were working normally.

"Hasn't the smell reached you yet?" I asked as I approached the manager.

"What smell?" he asked.

I explained that there was an awful smell at the far end of the main drawing office and that the area had to be cleared in order to remove the floorboards.

"You can't do that!" he exclaimed. "I don't believe it's necessary to go to that extent."

"Come and see, or rather smell, for yourself."

We walked down the office. There was absolutely no trace of the smell until we reached the last three metres of the office. We walked into it and quickly walked back. It was like walking into a curtain. There was a definite dividing line between smell and no smell.

"Yes, I see what you mean," he said. "Right, I will accommodate the draughtsmen at the other end of the office."

The joiner returned sometime later with the face masks. He and his mate stripped the office completely. The floorboards came up, the wall boards were taken off, and the ceiling was taken down. The whole of the last three metres of the office was stripped, cleaned, and disinfected and still the smell continued. For three days the joiner worked on that office, but all to no avail. The smell, that awful, dreadful smell, would not go away.

On the fourth day the smell started to move, I don't mean it started to go away. No, it started to creep up the office. A block of space some three metres long that contained the smell moved at a speed of about one metre every ten minutes slowly up the office. In half an hour the bottom of the office, where the smell had been originally, was clear. The entire office was evacuated, and it took five hours for the smell to travel the length of the office and disappear into the wall at the far end.

The fact that a smell of such strength should last over three days and then move the length of the office was strange enough, but what happened next was even stranger.

The next day the joiner started to rebuild the office. Everything seemed fine; the smell had gone and things were getting back to normal. That is, until my telephone rang at about nine-thirty. It was the nurse.

"Can you come to the first-aid room straight away?" she asked.

"Yes," I replied. "Anything wrong?"

"I'll tell you when you get here," she replied.

I went to the first-aid room. This room, which I have described earlier, was next door to the drawing office. I went in and the nurse was waiting.

"Just open that cupboard," she said.

I opened the medical cupboard on the wall. "Right. Now what?" I said.

"Just put your head a little way in."

This I did and I jumped back. The smell was in the cupboard. That same smell had taken refuge in the cupboard.

"Open a window," I said, "and I will open the cupboard. Leave it for an hour and see if it clears."

"Yes, all right," she said, "but that's a medicine cupboard. I will have to scrub it out when it's gone."

I returned to my office. An hour later the phone rang again.

"There's a terrible smell at the bottom of the stairs," someone said. I forget who it was.

I investigated and found the smell was on the move again. It had come out of the cupboard, out of the first-aid room, and was travelling up the stairs. It was moving a little faster this time. I went back to my office and waited.

As I expected, the phone never stopped ringing with people telling me about the smell. From the phone calls I could monitor the progress of the smell. It went up the stairs, across the inspection department, into the polish shop, and disappeared through the wall at the far end. I had never smelt such a smell before. If asked to describe it, I would have to say, "Rotting flesh." That is the best description I can give.

The smell became an annual event and would appear around September each year, last about three to four days and then move on the same route as it did the first time that I encountered it.

Another occasion when an office had to be demolished and rebuilt in a futile attempt to find an explanation happened sometime later. On this occasion it was the quality assurance manager's office, which was one of two offices directly above the old reception area. He came to me and asked if I would investigate noises in his office. I asked him to explain.

"I was working in my office late last night," he said, "and as far as I know I was the only person on the premises when there was a banging on the wall behind me."

"A banging," I said doubtfully.

"Yes," he said, "as though someone was hitting the wall with a hammer on the other side."

"That's a solid brick wall and it's an internal wall. There is only the ladies' toilet on the other side."

"I know," he said. "I went in there to see who it was, but there was no one there. I also went downstairs to the old reception area to see if anyone was banging on the wall down there, but there was no one else on site."

"That's strange," I said. "I'll come and have a look."

I went with him to his office and examined the wall in question. It was an internal wall that separated his office from the ladies' toilet. It was a solid brick wall, but it had been lined with plasterboard and painted. I tapped on the plasterboard.

"Did it sound like this?" I asked.

"No," he replied. "It was much heavier, as though someone was hitting brick with a heavy hammer."

I went into the ladies' toilet to look at the other side of the wall. This wall had been plastered and painted. There was no sign of hammer marks in the plaster work or any evidence at all of anyone hammering.

"I don't see what I can do," I said. "Let's leave it for now and see if it occurs again."

Two or three days later he complained of the banging again. "Could it be pipe work behind the plasterboard?" he asked.

"There are no pipes behind there," I replied.

"How about electric cables?"

"Yes, there are some cables, but they would only make a banging noise if there was a short circuit. Even then there would only be a single bang and the fuse or circuit breaker would cut the supply."

"Well, something is causing it," he said, "and it's getting on my nerves."

"I'll get the electricians to check the wiring, but I'm sure that isn't the cause."

I asked the electricians to check the wiring and look for any possible cause of the banging.

They checked the plug sockets, they went above the suspended ceiling, they checked everything they could, but nothing was found. I reported back to the quality assurance manager, telling him the only way to solve the mystery was to take down the plasterboard covering from the wall and examine the whole wall itself.

"I don't want to cause that much trouble," he said.

"Has anyone else heard the banging?" I asked.

"No, but I'm not imagining it," he replied.

"I'm not suggesting you are," I said, "but a second opinion is sometimes useful."

We left it at that and went about our business.

A couple of weeks later, a management meeting was called. All members of management were to meet in the works manager's office after working hours.

The works manager's office was next door to the quality assurance manager's office, the two separated by a partition made of plasterboard on a wooden frame and glass.

The members of the management, fifteen people in all, including myself, assembled in that office at 4:30 P.M.

The meeting got under way and was full of argument and debate as usual. At about 6:15, everyone stopped and listened. The debate had been disturbed by a loud hammering noise. It came from the office next door.

"There," said the quality assurance manager, a big smile on his face. "Now do you believe me?"

I left the meeting and went into his office. The banging had been very loud indeed, three bangs in all, and it came from the brick wall directly behind his desk.

I looked at the wall, went into the ladies' toilet, and went downstairs and checked there. Nothing! The factory was empty and no explanation for the noise was immediately apparent.

I returned to the meeting and promised that there would be a full investigation and I would conduct a detailed examination of the wall the very next day.

Next morning I asked the quality assurance manager to vacate his office while the work was going on. I had the joiner take the plasterboard off the wall, take the ceiling down, and completely expose the wall from floor to roof. Nothing, just a solid brick wall. No marks, no cracks, nothing. We satisfied ourselves that there was nothing wrong with the wall and rebuilt the office and redecorated it. No explanation of the banging was ever forthcoming, but as far as I know the banging was never heard again.

A rumour went around the factory regarding the banging and someone suggested that a works manager who used that office used to bang on the wall in order to tell the work force to finish their morning tea break and start work. Apparently, that same works manager had hung himself in that office. I investigated that story, but I could find no evidence to substantiate it, so I dismissed it as just speculation.

* * *

With all these incidents and reports, coupled with many smaller incidents, such as doors locking and unlocking themselves and lights switching themselves on and off, electric clocks that would only keep the correct time if placed in particular parts of the factory, a trolley, fitted with castors and fully loaded, revolving 180 degrees on a flat, level floor while two other people and I watched from ten feet away, I was beginning to be convinced that the place was haunted, as I had been told. I was finding it easier to believe than not to believe. Faced with overwhelming evidence, which I could not dispute, I began to find life was simpler if I believed. It did answer a lot of questions and I had more time to devote to the duties that I was paid to attend to and stop using my brainpower to try to find explanations, and yet . . . deep down inside me I still did not believe it. Putting all the reports and sightings to one side, ignoring my own experiences at that time, it just did not make any sense to me at all that a factory could be haunted and the vast majority of the work force accepted the hauntings as a fact of life, continuing as though nothing was happening, and no one had done anything about it. I found that I was becoming like two people. At the factory I would listen to reports and be totally convinced, but outside the factory I was completely the opposite and dismissed any such tales as complete nonsense.

At the factory I was still faced with being forced to give explanations for events that defied the basic laws of physics. For example, an object cannot move until a force is applied to it. Objects have often moved, but try to find the force! Impossible! You expect an extension light, fitted with a plug, to light up when it is plugged in and go out when it is unplugged. I have seen a light bulb stay on for several minutes after it has been unplugged. So many strange events that I was beginning to realise that most of them were happening to me. Yes, there were reports still coming in, but they were getting less and less, while the incidents I was witnessing were getting more and more.

One event that worried me at the time happened during the annual shutdown period. During these periods the factory closed completely with the exception of the maintenance crew and about five other people who had volunteered to help with the maintenance work for those two weeks. The men preferred to start early and finish early during the shutdown. This enabled them to take advantage of the long summer days spending the afternoons playing golf or spending time with their families during the school holidays. These men would start work at 6:00 A.M. and finish at 2:00 P.M. These hours were too early for me, and I would arrive at 7:30 A.M. and leave at 3:30 P.M. I would spend the last hour and a half checking on the progress of the maintenance work and planning the next day's activity. On my desk I would leave a schedule of the next day's work, which the supervisor would collect the next morning. Before I left I would walk through the building checking that all the lights were out and everything was locked. The watchman always waited until I left before he went home, but I felt happier if I had checked the security of the building myself.

On this occasion, it was around three-fifteen in the afternoon. I had walked the ground floor, and everything was secure. I spoke to Jim the watchman as I passed the main entrance.

"Are you off now?" he asked.

"Not yet, Jim," I replied. "I just want to check upstairs, I will only be ten minutes."

"Right," said Jim. "Give me a call when you leave and I'll lock the main door after you."

I went upstairs to the cabinet shop. This was the department where the furniture was made. It was a long room, about one hundred metres long. The first forty metres were narrower than the rest, about ten metres wide; the room then widened out to about thirty metres. The doorway to the flat-panel department was at the very bottom of the department, cut into the right-hand wall, and covered by a plastic strip curtain.

The whole area had a system of roller conveyors fastened to the floor in order to move the finished furniture easily over quite large distances. The furniture was placed on large wooden boards, the boards were placed on the conveyor rollers, and the furniture was pushed along the conveyors to the transport lift. It was then manually placed into the lift and taken downstairs for dispatch. The transport boards were then taken back to the work stations ready for the next piece of furniture. That was the theory. What happened in practise was that these boards were left anywhere and everywhere.

There was a clear walkway down the length of the cabinet shop from the stairs all the way down to the bottom end. There was another smaller lift at the bottom left-hand corner where the panels were brought up from the stores before being taken to the flat panel-department for lacquering and before assembly. These panels were transported by pallet trolleys, pushed by hand from the lift to the lacquering machinery.

I walked up the staircase and looked down the length of the cabinet shop. All the lights were out, but it was light enough to see on the bright sunny afternoon. The roof was fitted with skylights and there were windows all around the outside walls. The sun streamed through the skylights, illuminating the whole area.

The central walkway was clear with the exception of the transport boards, which were propped up against one side of the walkway. It was a habit of mine to walk to the bottom of the department, check the fire doors at the bottom end, and then walk back checking doors and windows on the way. On this occasion, I had walked about halfway down when a pallet trolley fully loaded with a pallet of panels moved from right to left slowly across the bottom of the cabinet shop. It had come from the vicinity of the flat-panel doorway and was heading towards the bottom lift. I stopped in amazement and watched it as it slowly went past the end of the walkway and came to rest some ten feet or so to the left. *Somebody's just pushed that,* I thought and ran down the cabinet shop into the flat-panel deparment. This area was darker and it took a few seconds for my eyes to get used to the darkness. There was no one there.

I stopped and listened for any sound that would tell me where they were. Nothing. I searched the area thoroughly. I found no one. The fire doors were locked on the inside. No one had got out that way. The windows were closed and fitted with stone guards, so exit through there would be impossible. Puzzled, I walked out of the area and over to the trolley that had caused me such anxiety. *It must have moved on its own for some reason,* I thought. I took hold of the handle and pushed. It did not move. I pushed again harder. The weight of the load must have been over half a ton. I pushed again with much effort, I just managed to get it moving. I pushed with all my strength, and then I let go of the handle. The trolley kept on moving for about two feet, and then it stopped. I had just seen it move on its own for over twenty feet.

I couldn't explain it, but no harm had been done, so I checked all the doors and proceeded to walk back down the cabinet shop the way I had come in, pausing to look again at the mysterious trolley. As I walked back I felt very uneasy. Nothing specific, just a sensation that I was not alone.

I was about halfway down when something happened behind me. I felt it rather than heard it: a draught of air hit me at the back of the legs. I jumped with the shock. Looking back, I smiled to myself. One of the transport boards, which had been propped up against the wall, had fallen over. A board that was made of half-inch plywood and measured two feet by four feet had fallen face-down across the aisle behind me. I walked back and picked it up. Putting it back in place, I turned and continued walking. There it was again—the blast of air hit my legs. I looked back and saw the board had fallen over again.

I'm not picking it up again, I thought. *Leave it.*

I started walking again and a blast hit me on the back of the legs once more. I didn't look back. I started walking quickly; then I started running.

When I reached the staircase, I turned left to go down the stairs. A quick glance back down the cabinet shop told me not one but up to twelve boards had fallen over in sequence as I had passed them. I had not touched them or knocked them in any way.

I quickly went down the stairs two at a time and went straight to the boiler house, where I knew Jim would be.

"What's up?" asked Jim, grinning all over his face. "You look like you have just seen one of the residents."

"I haven't seen anyone," I said, "but I have just seen a trolley move on its own and then the boards fell down in sequence as I walked past. It gave me quite a start."

"I've told you, strange things happen at this factory."

I sat down for a few seconds. When I recovered, I told Jim I was leaving.

"Right," said Jim, "I'll lock up after you, and then I'll go and pick up those boards you knocked over."

"I didn't—"I cut myself short. *What's the use trying to explain?* "Thanks, Jim. I'll see you in the morning." With that I left for home.

Something else happened during that very same shutdown. I did not think much of it at the time, but thinking back, I realise it was probably significant.

As I have said, the shutdown period was for maintenance work. One of the jobs that had to be done every shutdown was the stripping of the boilers. This had to be done for inspection purposes and was a legal requirement. The internal of the boiler had to be inspected by an independent inspector. He was appointed by the insurance company.

The boiler had been stripped and opened, ready for the inspection. I liked to do an inspection myself, just in case there were any obvious faults that could be rectified before the inspector arrived. I had my head inside an inspection hatch when I got the feeling that someone was behind me. I thought it was one of the lads wanting to ask me something.

"Hang on," I said, "I won't be a minute."

I carried on with what I was doing, and then I lifted myself out of the inspection hatch and turned round. They were not there. I caught a glimpse of someone just disappearing around the front of the boiler. I walked after him.

As I turned the corner I saw a little old man dressed in bib and brace–type blue overalls and a flat cap.

"Can I help you?" I asked the man, who was a stranger to me.

He didn't seem to hear me. He walked around the other side of the boiler. I followed. I turned the corner after him. He was not there. He had just vanished. There was no way out at that side and no easy path through, as the boiler was too close to the wall. He had just gone.

I went back to the electricians' workshop and told the electricians about it.

"Little bloke in a flat cap?" asked Graham. "I've seen him."

"Who is he?" I asked.

"No idea," replied Graham. "I've seen him walk past the gap between the two boilers. I've shouted and gone after him, but he's never there when you reach the spot where you last saw him."

"Not another ghost," I said disbelievingly.

"I'm not saying that," said Graham, "I'm just saying that I have often seen a little bloke in a flat cap and overalls and I have never caught up with him."

"Well, I've just seen him and he looked very real to me, but he wasn't there when I turned the corner," I explained.

"That happens every time," said Graham.

I left it at that.

I saw the little fellow on another occasion. I was up in the room above the coal bunker and the wood waste bunker. I was just about to climb down the ladder back to floor level when I saw him from above. He walked from the front of the small boiler down the side and around the back of the boiler. I lost sight of him as he walked out of my line of vision.

I came down the ladder and could find no trace of him. There was no way out, not from where I had last seen him.

Another incident happened in the boiler house the following winter. It has been mentioned earlier that there were coal-burning boilers in use at Old Castle Works in the mideighties. There were, in fact, two G. W. B. Vecos coal-burning boilers. The smaller of the two was used as a standby boiler when the larger one broke down. In the depths of winter, however, the old factory was so badly insulated that both boilers had to be used simultaneously. The two boilers were fuelled by a mixture of coal and sawdust. This was blown into the fire chamber by a powerful fan. The sawdust was collected from the woodworking machines and burnt to supplement the coal. This was an old, inefficient system, as the pressure of the air inside the firebox was far greater than the air pressure outside the boiler. Because of this, the door giving access to the fire chamber had to have a fireproof seal around the edge and needed to be bolted shut with a locking bar and two hand wheels. This door had to be sealed securely in order to prevent smoke, sparks, or even flames from blowing out into the boiler house. The seal on the door was made from an asbestos substitute fibre rope. In order to fit a new seal, it had to be soaked in water to make it flexible and then hammered into a recess that went all the way around the circular door. Once the rope was in position, the door would be closed, bolted, and locked, and the fire would then be lit. The heat from the fire would bake the seal in the exact shape of the boiler face and the door and so effect a seal. Once the baking had taken place the seal would become very hard, and it would remain in place until the following year, when it would be renewed.

Removal of the old seal, once it had baked hard, was quite a task. A fitter would have to use a hammer and chisel and chip away at it for several hours in order to remove it.

The incident happened, as I recall, at the beginning of February, in the depths of winter. Both boilers had been used every day since the factory reopened after the Christmas holidays. It was about 11:00 A.M. and I visited the boiler house to check that all was well.

During the day the watchman looked after the boilers, and it was his responsibility to report any small fault to me as soon as it became apparent, especially during the winter months.

"Everything OK, Jim?" I asked as I walked into the boiler house.

"Yes," replied Jim, "the boilers are doing well keeping pressure during this weather. The demand for heat right now is as high as you can get."

"Good," I said. "Let's hope it stays like that."

I checked the pressure; both boilers were at four bar. Coal had been delivered the day before, so we had plenty of fuel. Both doors were fully closed and bolted; the seals were doing their job. I looked through the observation spyhole in the doors; the fire was really blazing.

"It's nice to see everything running; let's hope it stays like that," I said.

"Yes, fingers crossed," replied Jim. "Do you fancy a coffee?"

"Yes, I think I'll have one with you," I replied.

We both left the boiler house and went to the coffee machine at the bottom of the stairs.

"White with?" Jim asked.

"That's right," I replied.

He put his money in and dialled the number. He passed the coffee to me, and I waited until he had collected his own. We both walked back from the machine together.

As we approached the boiler house, we could see smoke coming from beneath and around the boiler house door.

We opened the door and shut it again, quickly. The boiler house was full of smoke.

"What's going on?" asked Jim.

"There's a major problem with the boiler!" I cried.

"I'll go in and see," he said.

"No, you don't; you can't go in there."

"Someone has to switch them off," he argued.

“If someone is going in, I am,” I said. “Stay here and wait until I get back.”

Putting my coffee down, I put my handkerchief over my face and opened the door. I couldn’t let Jim go in; he was an old man and couldn’t move quickly enough. “Shut the door behind me!” I yelled.

As I opened the door, a cloud of greyish black smoke billowed out. Taking a deep breath, I dived inside. I knew the layout of the boiler house like my own backyard.

Inside, I couldn’t see a thing for the smoke, but I didn’t need to. I knew exactly where I was going.

I quickly went to the control panel for the large boiler. As I approached it I could just see the red light next to the emergency stop button. I hit it hard. The stop button was a mushroom-head type, and one hit in the directon of the red light was all that was needed. The next part was a little more difficult, I had to go around the back of the little boiler. The control panel for that one was around the other side.

I hit my shin on a pipe or something, and it hurt like hell. Have you ever wanted to cry out while holding your breath?

I didn’t have time to stop. I got around and hit the stop button on that control panel. The whine of the motors slowly getting less told me I had been successful. I quickly made my way back to the door. The whole episode had taken less than fifteen seconds.

I fell through the door and slammed it shut behind me. I felt the warm trickle of blood running down my shin. I bent over and looked at my leg.

“Now what have you done? Can’t leave you alone for five minutes,” joked Jim.

“Just banged my leg,” I said. “I’ll go and get cleaned up. You stay here; no one goes in that boiler house until

I get back." The smoke needed time to clear and we couldn't open the boiler house door yet without filling the factory with smoke.

I didn't bother sending for the nurse. I went back to my office to put a plaster on my cut. Brian, the maintenance supervisor, was there.

"What have you done?" he asked as I limped into the office.

"Oh, I have just bumped my leg," I replied, "but more important that that, there's something wrong with the boilers." I explained what had happened while I dressed my leg. We both returned to the boiler house. Jim was standing there.

"Has anyone been in there?" I asked.

"No one has got past me," he replied.

He cautiously opened the door. The smoke was beginning to clear. There were enough holes in the roof for it not to take long. I went in first, the others following close behind.

"Open the big outside door," I told Jim.

This he did while Brian and I looked for the cause of the smoke. It didn't take long. There was soot and ash all around the small boiler door.

"The seal's blown," said Brian.

"Looks like it," I replied. "Leave it for a few minutes for it to cool down before we open it.

"Jim, restart the other boiler."

Jim restarted the big boiler while Brian took a pair of heatproof gloves from out of the locker.

We waited a couple of minutes for the fire to die down, and then Brian opened the door.

The seal on the door had not blown; it was completely missing. We all looked on in complete astonishment. The seal was just not there. The recess where the seal had been was as clean as a whistle, not a trace that a seal had ever been there at all.

"Explain that," said Brian.

"I would not have believed it if I had not seen it for myself," I replied.

How can an asbestos-type seal be removed from a door that was bolted shut, as a fire at about one thousand degrees Celsius raged not six inches away? This all happened in less than five minutes' time, the time it took for Jim and me to walk to the coffee machine and back. Even if someone had come in, switched the boiler off, and physically removed the seal, it would have taken hours to remove it, and when that was done the seating would never have been as clean as it was now.

"You and Gary had better fit a new seal as quickly as possible," I said to Brian.

"Right," he replied. "I'll put one in water; it can be soaking while the boiler cools down."

This was done and the small boiler was back in action the following morning.

A few days later Jim came walking into my office, Brian was also there at the time.

"Look what I've found in the car park," Jim said, holding up the boiler door seal, still intact, forming a full circle the size of the boiler door.

"You found it where?" asked Brian.

"In the car park," said Jim.

We all examined the seal. It was fully intact; not a chisel mark or any damage at all was visible.

None of us wasted any brainpower on trying to find an answer. We just got on with the job.

Chapter 6

I began to take an interest in events that had been reported at other places—sightings and newspaper reports, television programmes, horror films, books, anything I could find to help solve the problem. Some of the reports I read told of some strange events, but nothing compared with what I was experiencing on a daily basis. One passage I read helped me a little way to opening my mind to acceptance. It said:

> Does the paranormal or the supernatural exist? If we accept that we have much to learn about the physical world and we do not as yet know everything there is to know, then it must follow that there are many things which can happen that we have no explanation for. Our knowledge as yet is not extensive enough to be able to answer everything. Therefore events can happen which cannot be explained by present-day knowledge and thus the paranormal must exist.

I was thinking about this when I had my first real experience of what it is like to be terrified, although I thought I behaved in a dignified manner. I pride myself that I was in total control of my behaviour throughout.

It was a Friday afternoon. The factory closed at 3:30 each Friday and the work force had left the factory today. I had about an hour's work to complete before I could leave and start the weekend. I was totally alone, sitting at my desk, going through some paperwork, my mind not completely on the job. My mind kept wandering to the unexplained. I was feeling a little tired, as I always do after a week's work, and I had to keep forcing myself to get on with the boring task of sorting through the week's invoices.

My office had windows on two sides that looked straight out into the workshop. Most of the workshop lights had been switched off. Only one had been left on, for me to find my way out of the workshop when I had finished. The door of my office was at the far left-hand side. From my desk I could see directly into the workshop.

It was strange sitting there in an empty workshop; the silence seemed to close in on me. I was used to the workshop being noisy and full of activity. Sitting there alone in a factory said to be haunted did not give me a feeling of being totally secure. I told myself to get on with the job. The sooner it was finished, the sooner I could be home.

I had gone on with the work, going through the invoices, sitting with my head down and writing on the paper in front of me, when I got the feeling that I was being watched.

I did not look up or move my head, I continued writing, but the feeling did not go away. Staring at the paper in front of me, I sat motionless. I did not dare look up.

After a few moments I dared to move my eyes, without moving my head. I lifted my eyebrows to give a clearer line of vision.

There's someone at the window, I thought.

My heart started beating faster. I still made no movement. I could only see the bottom third of the window, and a figure definitely stood there. I quickly looked back down to my desk. My mind started racing. *What to do? What to do?*

Do nothing, I told myself. *Carry on with what you are doing; pretend you haven't seen him.*

Without lifting my head, I reached to my left and pulled another invoice in front of me.

It could be one of the lads trying to give me a fright. Well, he's succeeded, I thought. *Ignore him; don't give him the satisfaction.*

I continued looking at the paper in front of me. My hands were on the desk, a pen in one of them. I pretended to write on the paper.

Staring down, I could see the veins in my hand getting larger. My blood pressure was rising. A feeling of terror was beginning, growing below my lower rib cage.

I ventured another look—a quick glance, that was all.

It's still there. Go away; go away.

I was beginning to get very hot now, my shirt collar was getting tighter, and I could feel the vein in the side of my neck pulsing. Still I did not move; I just stared at the paper in front of me. A pain started in my lower back, in my kidneys, the adrenaline starting to flow.

I can't sit here much longer.

My self-control was reaching breaking point.

Look up and face it, I said to myself. *NO I CAN'T! I CAN'T!* The pain in my back got worse. *Do it. . . . Do it. . . . NOW!*

With that I looked up and my eyes met a sight that had been described to me so many times.

I wanted to scream, to cry out, anything to relieve the pressure I felt within. I didn't. I looked in horror at a figure—well, not a figure, an empty monk's habit of dark, rough material with an empty hood staring at me.

I wanted to run, dive under the desk, move, anything, but I didn't, I couldn't.

I stared back at it. Not through choice. I couldn't move. I couldn't even blink my eyes. I just froze, the hair on the back of my neck bristling. We stared at each other for several seconds. Slowly the figure began to fade. At first it seemed solid and real; then it slowly became transparent, until it finally disappeared altogether.

Still staring at the window, I finally sat back in my chair. I breathed deeply and began to relax. The feeling of terror inside my stomach remained, but my heart rate began to return to normal and the pain in my back began to subside. My head started spinning. Was I going to faint?

No, I will not faint. I have never fainted in my life. I will not faint now, I said to myself. *Calm down; calm down. It's gone. Come on; breathe deeply; breathe, breathe.*

I took deep breaths again and again.

I finally returned to normal, but it took a long time.

When I had recovered enough, I plucked up courage and quickly walked out of the building, not stopping to switch off the lights or lock any doors. I ran across the road and got into my car. There I sat for a good ten minutes before I felt I was safe to drive.

I live about an hour's drive away from the factory, and before I arrived home I was beginning to doubt the evidence of my own eyes. Did I really see a hooded figure or was I dreaming? Did I fall asleep at my desk and dream the whole thing? I decided not to tell anyone, not even my wife. I did not want to frighten her or for her to be afraid for my sake. No, I would not tell anyone until I was sure of what I had seen or until such time that it did not matter anymore.

That weekend I was very quiet and withdrawn, deep in thought, trying to sort it all out. The more it went through my mind, the more confusing it became. I came to a decision: to treat the episode just as a bad experience, not to dwell on it too much, as it must have been a dream.

The memory of dreams usually fades with time. The memory of this event was and is vivid. I can remember the figure in great detail, and the feelings that I experienced at the time come back to me whenever I think of the event.

Monday morning came and I arrived back at the factory as usual. I tried to behave normally. I did, however, avoid sitting in my office until well into the afternoon. When finally I did sit down I became very nervous every time someone passed by the window. I would jump and my blood pressure rose again.

I began wondering who the hooded figure was. Was it an earthbound spirit, as the books I had read had suggested, or something else? I must know, I must find out, but how? This thought became an obsession. I racked my brains to find out who it was. Local historians could tell about the area back to Cromwell's time, and also who the monastery belonged to and who gave them the land, but any information on the monks themselves was not forthcoming, with the exception of the fact that they were self-sufficient and grew licorice on the local land.

The one thing I was convinced about was, if I accepted that the place was haunted, then the figure I had seen was not "Charlie." I was absolutely certain of that. Who was it? What was it? Were there more of them? Was the factory the meeting ground for all the unearthly spirits and ghosts who had no other place to go? The questions were endless. I was soon to find out, but not by the method that I had imagined I would.

It happened several days later. I was in the middle of a conversation when a picture appeared, flashing into my mind. It took me totally by surprise. I stopped mid-sentence.

"Is something the matter?" I was asked. I could hear the voice, but it was as though he were far away.

"Peter, is something wrong?" he said. The voice seemed strange, full of echoes. The person I had been speaking to grabbed my arm. This brought me back to my senses.

"What? What?" I said

"You had better go and sit down; you look terrible."

"Yes, I don't feel too good," I replied. "I'll go back to my office. Sorry. I'll speak to you later."

I made my way back to my office, but the picture was still in my mind. It was like having a dream, but I was wide awake. I knew what I was doing, but inside my head, the right side of my head, was this picture—no, not a picture, a scene, as though I was watching a film. It was as though my brain was in two halves. With the left side, I was in complete control of my thoughts, movement, my entire function, but the right side had this scene with people and places I had never seen before. I was stuck between two worlds.

As I walked back to my office, people spoke to me and I answered them, although their voices sounded distant. My own voice seemed normal, and I knew precisely what I was doing and where I was going. Sitting down in my office chair, alone in my office, I concentrated on the scene in my head.

The scene was of the area long before the factory was built. I recognised the church. It was still in the position it is now, but not a ruin. I was looking at the scene from above water. A wall ran across the front of the scene, a large wall made of blocks of golden-coloured stone. In the background were hills with trees, forests. I was somehow looking at this scene from about six feet above the water level. I was above the dam. As I turned my head, the scene changed with it; it was as though I was there, watching. I turned and looked at the castle. It was magnificent, not like I had imagined it at all, made of gold-coloured stone and towering formidably above me to the right. There was a wooden cross in the water, a little way in front of me, to the left. It had been planted into the bottom of the dam, so the crosspiece was about two feet above the water level. It was about twenty feet away from the dam wall, and it was made of clean round sections of wood. The crosspiece had been rebated into the upright and bound with strong rope. The section of upright above the crosspiece was only about twelve inches high.

A procession of monks was walking along the wall. The wall itself was about four or five feet wide and flat and level along the top. At the end of the wall, to the right, was a small building. There was an archway in the wall just before the building, which had a door or gate in front of it. Ropes were attached to the gate and tied to wooden posts set into the wall.

The procession walked over the archway heading towards the left-hand side of the dam. Two of the monks were following the procession on a raft in the water, pushing themselves along with poles. The monks walked slowly two by two along the wall. One man walked along on his own; he was number five in the line. When number five was opposite the cross, the file nearest the water stopped. The second file walked past and stopped. They turned towards the water. They stood there for a few

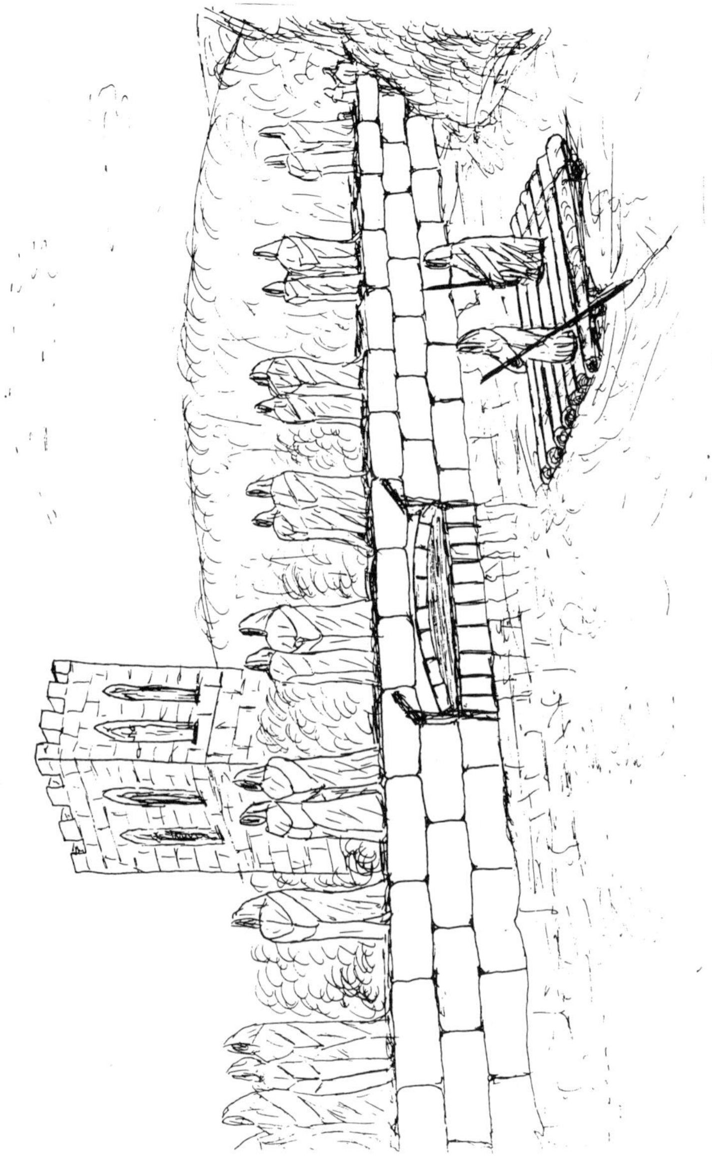

minutes until the monks on the raft came level with number five.

The two monks on either side of number five removed his habit and threw it onto the raft. The raft then started to make its way to the cross. When the raft reached the cross, the two monks put the habit onto the cross, putting the arms of the habit over the crosspiece, and the hood was lifted up onto the upright. They dressed the cross with the habit as a scarecrow would be dressed.

While this was happening number five was standing totally naked. The monks who had removed his habit produced some rope and began to bind his legs together. Number five offered no resistance. The raft made its way back to the wall. Number five was lowered gently onto the raft. There was no resistance and no force was used. It was done with the full cooperation of the person concerned. The raft once again moved towards the cross. The three men stood very still as they made their way across the water. On reaching the cross, number five held out his arms and one of the monks tied two pieces of rope, one to each of number five's wrists. They were tied firmly, and the long ends were left hanging, one from each arm. The three men stood up, and number five turned with his back to me. The two other monks stood on either side of him, facing me. They took hold of the ropes and jumped in the water, pulling number five in after them, backwards.

The monks swam towards the cross. Number five disappeared from sight; he could not swim with his legs bound together. Both monks pushed their piece of rope down the sleeves of the habit, wrapped it around the crosspiece, and pulled, hard. Number five shot out of the water, and his arms were pulled down the sleeves of the habit. The monks proceeded to tie the him to the cross.

One monk swam back to the raft, reached up and took another length of rope from the raft, and swam back to the cross. He dived under the water, where he bound number five to the cross; round and round he swam until number five was fully secured. The two swam back to the raft, climbed aboard, and moved off to the right in the direction of the shore. The monks on the wall stood looking for a while, then turned and walked off in single file, back the way they had come. Number five was left hanging on the cross, his head and face clear of the water. I could see from the side view I had that he was not in distress; he just hung there in the water, his eyes closed and his head bowed.

Then the scene was gone; it just went, as though someone had just shut a door or turned out a light. Occasionally I thought the scene had returned, but I realised it was only the memory of the event, not the scene itself, that I was seeing.

The next day or the day after—I don't remember exactly—I was walking down the road outside the factory. It was around ten in the morning. Suddenly the scene came back. Not like before: this time I was walking along the wall. It was a strange sensation, difficult to describe. My eyes were seeing the roadway and the factory, but the picture in my head, the right side of my head, was of the dam and the dam wall. Again the scene changed as I walked or moved my head. It was as though I had a third eye, which was looking into the past. This time the scene lasted only a few seconds. I stopped, turned, and looked back.

The monk on the cross in the water was still there. This time I was seeing him from the dam wall. He was looking at three monks on the wall some twenty feet or so from me. They were throwing food to him. He was trying to catch the food in his open mouth. They were throwing what looked like bread and pieces of meat. A piece of meat hit him in the face and stuck to his cheek. I watched as he manoeuvred his head in order to get it into his mouth. It was like feeding the ducks, I thought, and then the scene was gone.

This was the first time I had experienced anything outside the factory walls. The memory of what I had seen kept coming back, but I had to carry on as normal. I had a job to do, and I was not going to let pictures in my head stop me from doing it.

The next time the scene returned, I was on the wall looking straight at the monk on the cross. It was horrible. He was hanging there, his flesh becoming a very light shade of grey. His head was hanging, and his hands were like two wrinkled grey leather gloves. There were several large black crows or ravens flying around him. One of the birds landed on his head, which was bowed forward, the hood of the habit upright, with the cross supporting it. The bird leaned forward and down. PECK, PECK, it went at his face. It was pecking his eyes out.

OH NO, I thought. *I hope he's dead.*

The head gave a slow sideways movement, and the bird flew off.

He's still alive; he's being eaten alive by the local wildlife. I don't want to look anymore, I thought. *No more, no more,* but the scene would not go away.

I turned my head so I could not see him. The large black bird circled overhead, then another, and another. I tried not to turn back to look at him, but I could not prevent myself. I turned and looked. His head was lifted up now; he was directly facing me. His eyes were gone. Large, red, empty sockets stared at me with blood running down his cheeks. There were open sores on the side of his head, and his lips were black, with skin hanging off.

I wanted to help him. Oh! How I wanted to help, but how could I? I wasn't even there. I looked down into the water. I could see what was left of his feet, through the crystal clear water. They had swollen to twice their size. They did not look like feet anymore, just lumps of swollen rotten flesh. The skin had peeled off and was hanging down in streamers, which floated to and fro with the gentle movement of the water. Then the scene was gone.

I was severely distressed with what I had seen. What had this poor man done? Had he committed some crime? Why had they left him there to die? Why was I seeing it? This wasn't my imagination. In your imagination you can change what you don't like. You can stop thoughts that upset you. I had no such control. The scenes appeared and disappeared at intervals without my being aware of how or when they appeared.

The next time I saw that poor, poor man, he was dead. It was a hot summer day. A swarm of flies was around what was left of his head. His hands were gone. The bones of his fingers were just hanging from the ends of his sleeves. His head was bowed right down, his face almost touching the surface of the water. Something fell from his head and made a gentle splash in the water, the ripples forming circles that continually moved outwards.

I looked at the top of his head, which was facing me, the hood of the habit still standing upright in the hot summer sun. On the top of his head were holes in the skin. Something moved. MAGGOTS—his head was a mass of heaving, wriggling, disgusting maggots. The white of his skull caught the sunlight, brilliant white patches occasionally exposed by the movement of the vile insect larvae. The sight made my stomach turn; I was going to be sick. I ran to the gents' toilet, the scene still in my mind. I ran into the cubicle. There I was physically, dreadfully, sick. I vomited until my stomach ripped with the pain of heaving. The scene left my mind. I sat down in the cubicle and wept. I wept like I had never wept before in my life. *How could man treat his fellow man that way? This diabolical deed had been committed by monks, men of a religious order. How could they do it? Why did they do it?*

As I thought this, my sorrow turned to anger. I left the cubicle, the feeling of anger welling up inside me. I did not feel ill anymore. I wanted to hit something. I wanted to get to those men; I wanted to destroy them and make them pay for what they had done to that poor man. I wanted revenge for him. But how could I? It all probably happened six hundred years ago.

The feeling of anger and frustration was unbearable. I just started walking around and around the six-acre site the factory occupies. I walked for about two hours.

When finally I calmed down I made the decision to shut it out of my mind, occupy myself with something else, tell no one, do nothing as if there was anything I could do! Just get on with my work, bury myself in my work, do not think about it at all. If only it had been as easy as that!

The scene appeared only once more to me after that. It was sometime later—I don't remember how long. It took me completely by surprise as it had done the other times.

This time it was autumn, the wind was blowing, and the water of the dam was splashing up the dam wall. I was standing on the wall again. The sky was dark and cloudy. The castle on the hill above me now looked dark and depressing. I looked towards the spot twenty feet out from the wall. The cross was still there, but the body of the monk was not; all that was left was the monk's habit.

I recognised it straightaway. This was what I had seen in the workshop that Friday evening. It was exactly as I remembered it, only the arms were outstreched to the side, supported by the wooden cross. The empty hood looked at me then exactly as it had done before.

The scene did not suddenly diappear this time. It gradually faded, became transparent, and finally disappeared altogether. It never appeared to me again.

Was that the answer? Had I and all those other people seen the spirit of the poor, wretched monk who died in such a slow, tortured way all those years ago? If it was and I saw it again, I would not be afraid this time. In fact, I would probably go to him, put my arm around him, and tell him that at least somebody cared, somebody knew how he had died, and someone at least felt sorrow and remorse that he should have met his fate in such a terrible way.

There have been no more sightings of that hooded figure; at least none as reported to me. I have only once seen a monk's habit since and the circumstances following that incident led me to wish I hadn't.

*   *   *

After such a traumatic experience, I was in total state of confusion. I did not know what to believe and what not to believe. Something had shown me those pictures; something had answered those questions I had been puzzling over. One thing I knew for certain. I don't know how I knew; I just did. The monk who had died all those years ago was not Charlie. But if he wasn't, who, where, what was Charlie? Was he a friend or enemy? Was I becoming possessed?

Something had put those scenes in my head. I hadn't and I had no control over them. It's a frightening thought that someone or something has access to your mind. I didn't like it, I didn't like it at all, but what could I do about it? Leave my job, run away, never come back? These solutions were always a possibility.

Solutions? Did I say solutions?

Running away was not a solution. I am not the type to run away, I never have been. Stay and fight, that's what my instinct says.

Fight? Fight what? I did not need to fight anything. I had not been harmed; no one had. I had been harassed, tormented, teased, and played with, like a man plays with his dog, but no harm had come to me and no harm would come to me if I could master this fear within me. Fear of the unknown, that's what I had to fight.

I became resolved to fight the fear. Fear had been a stranger to me. I had never experienced fear, real fear, before. I had been nervous and been in situations that I would rather not have been in but the fear I felt when I saw that monk's habit was a completely new experience for me. I hope I never experience it again. I was determined not to. This fear was what I was going to fight.

I set about doing this by forcing myself to be alone in the factory and just sit there in the dark. I had, on occasion, to return to the factory in the early hours of the morning because of a problem with the heating system, a call out for security reasons, a break-in, or whatever. I would use these occasions to walk alone through the factory. I would particularly walk through the areas where the sightings or other things had happened. I found, eventually, that I could do this easily—quite confidently, in fact. I never saw anything and nothing happened to me, except I conquered the fear.

Chapter 7

The fire alarm system here had been quite sophisticated for an old factory. It had a sprinkler system and an electrical break-glass alarm system. The two systems were linked together by a pressure switch. The sprinkler system was filled with water and pressurised by the means of a pump to 80 psi. In the event of a fire, the sprinkler head would burst, due to the heat, and the pressurised water would spray onto the fire. When the pressure in the system dropped by 15 psi the pressure switch would activate and the alarm system would sound. When the alarm sounded, an auto-dial system would dial the fire brigade, on a private phone line, and a recorded message would play over the telephone. It would repeat, "Fire, fire, fire," followed by the name and address of the company. The tape would rewind and the microprocessor would dial the next number in the memory and the procedure would be repeated. The telephone numbers were programmed into the memory and could only be dialled automatically in strict rotation. It was also impossible for the numbers to be dialled without the fire alarms sounding. My home phone number was the second in the memory. If a fire occurred, the auto-dial system would notify the fire brigade ant then it would notify my home.

If anyone has an explanation for the events you are about to be told, I would be happy to listen to it.

I had to be at work at 7:30 each morning. I arose at 5:30 and left home an hour later in order to get there on time. This particular morning it was 6:25 and I was just putting on my coat, getting ready to leave, when the phone rang. My wife was already awake and was walking downstairs as I picked up the receiver. A voice boomed out, "Fire, fire, fire, there is a fire at—"

I didn't need to listen any further. I knew what came next.

"I've got to rush," I said to my wife. "There's a fire at work."

"Don't drive too fast," she said as I left.

Off I went. I drove as quickly as I could to the factory. It normally takes an hour, but I made it in fifty minutes. I arrived at 7:15.

"Where's the fire brigade? Why is everyone walking into the factory?"

I went straight to the boiler house to find the watchman. "Where was the fire?" I asked thinking they had been and gone before I arrived.

"What fire?" asked Jim.

"I received the recorded message at home just before 6:30," I said. "The fire alarms must have sounded for me to get the call."

"There have been no fire alarms and no fire here," replied Jim. "Everything's been quiet."

"That's impossible," I said. "I got the call."

Brian, the maintenance supervisor, arrived on the scene at that moment. "You're early," he said as he walked up.

"Brian," I said, "I got a fire call at home and so I rushed to get here."

"Fire? What fire?" he asked.

As he spoke, the long low wail of the siren started up. Its tone was low at first but quickly built up into an ear-splitting scream.

"That fire," I replied.

With that we quickly ran to the fire assembly point. Brian grabbed the roll call list from the wall of the boiler house as we passed. We went through the procedure of calling the names on the list and making sure everyone was out of the factory.

The fire engines arrived within three minutes. I walked across the road to the fire chief.

"Where's the sprinkler valve?" he asked.

We both went to the main entrance. I showed him where the valve was. There were two sprinkler systems, one with the pipes painted red and the other with the pipes painted blue.

"Which system has been activated?" he asked.

A quick look at the pressure gauges told me. "The red system," I said.

"Where does that run?"

"Straight ahead," I replied. "The red system covers the road side of the factory, upstairs and down; the blue covers the lower half."

"Thanks," he said. "You go back across the road and leave us to it. I'll call you if you are needed."

I returned to the assembly point. Brian had completed the roll call by then.

"Everyone present?" I asked.

"As far as I know," he replied. "It's difficult at this time in the morning. I don't know whether they are somewhere around or just late for work."

"Well, the fire brigade is in charge now. It's not as though the whole place is going to go up," I said. "Watch for latecomers and stop them from going into the factory."

There was a lot of activity along the roadway at the far end of the factory.

"It looks like the fire is in the sports room," I said to Brian.

"Looks like it," he replied. "At least we know there is no one in there. It's kept locked, apart for special events and the lunch hour."

"Was anything happening in there last night?" I asked.

"No," he replied. "There hasn't been an evening session for a couple of weeks."

We watched as the firemen ran backwards and forwards, running their hoses out and shouting orders to each other.

After a short time the fire chief came looking for me. "It's safe to go back in now." he called.

"Send them all back in," I repeated to Brian.

"What caused it?" I asked the fire chief.

"Come and have a look," he replied. "An electric storage heater overheated and ignited the wallpaper behind it, which in turn ignited the woodwork, and so on."

"Much damage?" I asked.

"No," he replied. "You've been lucky. There is no structural damage at all, just decoration and the studding wall mainly."

We walked into the sports room; there was not a lot of damage. An old electric storage heater, which had been placed against a partition wall, had overheated as the fire chief had described. The thermostat on the heater had failed to switch off the electric supply, and the old heater had become hotter and hotter until it finally ignited the partition behind it.

The fire brigade left and work in the factory resumed. Everything got back to normal, leaving me to organise the restoration of the sports room.

Half an hour later, when I had organised everything, Brian asked, "How did you know about the fire?"

"I told you," I said. "I got a fire call from the auto-dial system."

"But you couldn't have," he replied. "The alarms and sprinklers didn't go off until an hour later, and you were here then."

"I know," I said, "but my wife was there and she heard it, too. I'll call her and see if there was another call at 7:30." This I did and no, there had not been another call.

"So," said Brian, "let's recap the facts. Your number is second on the auto-dial memory. The auto-dial can only be activated by the same electric supply that sounds the fire alarms. The fire alarm can only be switched on if someone breaks a fire-point glass or the sprinkler system loses pressure. And yet the auto-dial phoned your house without the sprinklers losing pressure, without the fire alarms sounding, and without the auto-dial system phoning the fire brigade first."

"Absolutely correct," I said.

"Impossible," he replied.

"It happened, Brian. My wife heard me take the call, and I spoke to you and the watchman of the incident before any of us knew that there was a fire."

"I know," said Brian. "I believe you, but it's still impossible."

Both he and I racked our brains to come up with an answer. Had a fire break-glass point been activated? Brian did a full inspection of all the fire points in the factory; all were intact. Had the heat from the fire somehow melted the wiring of the fire alarm system just enough to make a split-second contact, which activated the auto-dial system and then somehow dialled the second number first? It then would switch off, because the fire brigade was first in the memory and the system needed to be reactivated before it went back to the top of its memory stack. Brian and I checked the wiring of the alarm system. The route of the cable, which was fireproof cable and cannot melt, did not go anywhere near the point of the fire. Try as we might, and this time the investigation was a joint effort, we could not find an explanation. We never have and the mystery remains.

How did I receive a phone call from an electrical mechanical device an hour before I should have? The system worked perfectly when the fire broke out. The sprinklers put the fire out, and as the pressure dropped the fire alarms sounded. The auto-dial system phoned the fire brigade, but the next thing should have happened was a phone call to my home. Somehow the last event on the list happened one hour before everything else.

* * *

Fire played a major part in yet another event, again in the flat-panel department. This department, as I have explained earlier, was where the finished wooden panels were coated with lacquer. This was done by placing the panels on conveyor belts, which carried the panels through a series of machines. Each machine had a different function, but together they coated, dried, sanded, and final-coated the panels with lacquer.

The last machine in the line was called a curtain coater. This machine worked by pumping the lacquer from a tank into a trough situated above the conveyor. The trough had a slot in the bottom along the full length of it. This slot could be varied in width by the means of a mechanical adjusting wheel. The idea was that when the trough was full, the slot could be opened up and a curtain of lacquer would fall through a gap in the conveyor system and be caught in a tray and returned to the tank. The pump kept the trough full, and this formed a curtain, or wall, of lacquer. The panels were passed through this curtain at speed and a thin, even coating of lacquer was obtained without brush or roller marks on the finished surface.

The problem with treating panels in this way was that the lacquer was highly flammable. It needed a lot of thinners to give the correct viscosity to the lacquer for the curtain coater to function correctly. The lacquer was always being spilt, and even though the men cleaned up every day, a coating of lacquer built up on the floor and on the machinery.

A drive motor for one of the conveyors was directly under the machine. The area was a high-risk area for fire, and all the electric motors had to be flameproof. Even static electricity was catered to, as a spark from the fast-moving conveyor belts could cause a problem.

The fumes that built up in the area were so strong that air extraction equipment was used to reduce the explosive potential of the solvent vapour.

It had been a cause for concern that if a fire did break out in the area, with the buildup of fumes, an explosion was very likely. On this particular morning a fire did break out. The man who spotted it first was fully aware of the procedure. In fact, he was the union health and safety representative. A motor directly beneath the curtain coater suddenly burst into flames. He hit the break-glass fire alarm point and ran. Seeing him running, everyone ran, out of the building and to the fire assembly point. I heard the alarm go, and as the person in charge of such things, I immediately phoned the fire brigade. This was the normal procedure in the event of a fire. Not relying on the auto-dial system, anyone not in immediate danger should call the emergency service.

I quickly left the factory and joined everyone else at the assembly point. The fire brigade arrived and quickly went to the flat-panel department. Smoke by now had quickly built up and was filling the factory.

The firemen put on breathing apparatus and went into the area to fight the fire. The firemen quickly tackled the fire with a dry powder fire extinguisher.

After waiting a few minutes for the smoke to clear, the work force went back into the factory to resume work.

The maintenance crew and I went to assess the damage to the machines, in particular the conveyor belt. The belt was made of a rubber material with a canvas backing. To our surprise, the conveyor belt was untouched, not a mark on it, not even a blackening from the smoke. Pleased but puzzled about this, I told the electricians to remove the motor and take it back to the workshop for examination. When the motor was in the workshop, the white powder from the fire extinguisher was removed. We could see there was no sign whatsoever of the motor having been in a fire. It was covered with lacquer from the many spillages, but no evidence that it had been in a fire at all. It could not have been the motor that had been on fire; it must have been something else. A full examination of all the machines in the department was carried out by the full maintenance team, including myself. There was absolutely no sign that a fire had ever occurred at all, no smoke damage, no molten lacquer, nothing. I had not seen the fire myself, but the flat-panel men saw it, the firemen saw it, and the smoke that filled the factory was seen by everyone.

Yet another unexplained mystery for my files.

* * *

I think that it was these last two events, which happened within a short space of time of each other, that finally convinced me there was something in the factory that could not be explained by the laws of science. The machine breakdowns could be attributed to the lack of expertise on my part or the lack of understanding of how the machines function on the part of the maintenance department, the sightings could be imagination or part of some unknown mental disorder, the footsteps could be sounds made by other means that no one found, the smells and the banging wall could be part of some subterranean disturbance, but the intervention to events that could have destroyed the complete factory convinced me that something more powerful was watching over the site. This something, which I had called Charlie, was real and it was protecting the whole site. In particular, it was looking after me. From that moment I knew that Charlie was a friend and ally.

There was another event that could be put down to evidence of something looking after the site and the people. I will admit that this could have been a remarkable coincidence, a twist of fate, or whatever. In any event, it probably saved the lives of two of our women workers.

Above the sports room, at the far end of the factory, was the works canteen. This section of the building was buit in the 1960s, and so it was regarded as a new section of the factory. It was a two-storey building. Downstairs it formed part of the workshop area and the sports room, while on the upper floor were the showroom and the canteen. It was a brick structure with a steel framework.

The steel girders held up the precast concrete slabs that formed the upper floor and the roof. The building therefore had a flat roof, which was fitted with skylights. It was at the time the newest and best section of the factory. That is why it was used as the showroom and the canteen.

In order for the company to prepare food for consumption by the employees, it was subject to rigorous inspections by the local public health inspectors. No deterioration to the fabric of the building could be allowed, and the cleanliness and decoration had to be kept to a high standard. There were two ladies who worked in the canteen preparing food for the work force. They would start work at 8:30 A.M. and prepare sandwiches for the ten o'clock break, and then they would cook lunch for the work force, whose lunch hour is from twelve to one, and for the staff, whose lunch hour is from one until two. The ladies would clean up after the lunches were over and leave work at three o'clock.

In the workshop directly below was the upholstery section. There were only two people who worked in that area and there was no machinery, so the place was relatively quiet. On this particular day at three-twenty in the afternoon Bill, one of the men from the upholstery section, came walking into my office.

"I think you had better take a look and see what has happened in the canteen," he said as he walked into my office.

"Why? What happened?" I asked.

"A few minutes ago there was a tremendous crash from the floor above," he replied. "I've been upstairs and everything in the showroom looks all right, but the canteen is locked. I can't get in there."

"A crash?" I said. "What kind of a crash?"

go out, there was no fault with the switch, and the light still stayed on with the main supply switched off and the wiring disconnected. Even then the electrician would think that there was probably a short circuit and the power to light the bulb was coming from another source. If the bulb stayed lit when it was removed from the socket, then and only then would it be put on the list of unexplainable events. When the electrician tried to explain what had happened to the person who first reported that the light would not go out, he would not be believed.

This event and many others actually happened. The problem with the unexplainable is that if the events are of a technical nature only a technician can decide whether they are explainable or not. The average non-technical person would not realise that something that was normally impossible was happening.

Charlie is beyond tangible explanation. He (I prefer to refer to Charlie as *he*) is, as far as I can tell, pure energy. He has no physical form, but he has intelligence far above that of humans. He can move objects, create changes in temperature, create noises, and make highly technical machinery behave in the most bizarre fashion. He can make contact by putting pictures into the minds of anyone who is responsive enough to receive them. He can project images and create or remove any physical object he chooses. He cannot or does not seem to be able to move through space. The extent of his powers seems to be limited to a small section of land, which is contained within the six-acre site. It would not surprise me if, now I have written this, Charlie will prove me wrong by making something happen away from the site, but up and until now this has not happened. He does, however, seem to have the ability to move through time. This may make some kind of sense. If it does, it is the only thing that does. Our measurement of time is by movement through space: the Earth around the sun, the pendulum of a clock, the movement of the hands of a clock. Could it be that if there were no movement through space, then there would be no measurement of time and, therefore, time would not exist? This is getting too deep for the scope of this book. I will leave that for further discussion by people more qualified than I.

For now I can only say that Charlie has helped me many times and to me he is a friend. He has caused me pain and immeasurable mental anguish, but perhaps I, in some way, have benefited from the experiences. I must say, however, that these experiences are ones I could have well done without.

Chapter 8

It was about this time that I began to be known as the man with all the answers. I would be consulted about almost everything from engineering problems to complex production procedures. It all began in the management meetings. Problems that were put forward for discussion were debated and argued with no practical solution becoming apparent. I would suddenly speak up with a proposition that was met with the word, "Brilliant." Where did the idea come from? I don't know. As I spoke, the words seemed to be coming from someone else.

Normally, before I speak I think through what I am going to say. Not on this or subsequent occasions. This happened time and again at various meetings. My reputation and standing in the eyes of the directors grew rapidly.

One afternoon, in the middle of August, I was called to the managing director's office.

"Come in," he said. "Sit down."

I sat down in one of the chairs beside the boardroom table.

"To come straight to the point," he said, "the board of directors have decided to open a metalwork factory to supply all the metalwork that this company now buys from outside suppliers. I want you to take charge of the whole project. I will select a green field site, and I want you to supervise the building of the new factory, the selection and installation of the machinery and equipment, the tooling up and proving of the production procedures, the selection and training of the work force."

"I'm very flattered," I replied, "but I have no experience of setting up a factory from scratch. Who will be working with me?"

"From what I and the other directors have seen of your abilities, you can easily handle this project," he replied, "and will need no assistance from anyone. Myself and the other directors are here if you do need to talk over any problems or need advice on anything."

"Who will be standing in for me as works engineer?" I asked.

"No one," he replied. "I am sure you can handle both tasks together."

From his manner I could tell that I was not expected to refuse the assignment.

After further, detailed discussion, I left his office. It seemed that the directors had such confidence in my abilities that it didn't seem to matter that I had no experience in setting up a factory.

The building work started in January on a site less that half a mile from Old Castle Works. On the first of June the production of metal work for the furniture factory began. From start to finish in less than six months, not bad for a beginner.

I was asked to run the metal factory until a suitable factory manager could be found. I had to split my time between the running of the metal factory and being works engineer at the furniture factory. This I did, trying to get back to the furniture factory at least once a day. This was where all my ideas were hatched, where my inspiration came from. I am claiming the ideas and solutions as my own because there is no one else to claim them, but the ideas came from the same spot in my head where the scene of the monk's death had appeared.

The splitting of my time between the two factories lasted for just over a year. A manager for the metal factory was found and I was to resume my full-time positon as works engineer, but I had to start to pull down the old factory and rebuild on the same site without any disruption to production or interference with fulfilling of customer's orders. Not an easy thing to do, but demolition of the stores area began in August. The piece parts were stored in large marquees in the car park.

The old stores was demolished, the site cleared, the new building built, heating and lighting installed, and racking erected. This was all achieved in less than five months. The piece parts were back in the new stores and the marquees dismantled before the start of the Christmas holidays.

How did I achieve this all on my own? I had had no experience before the metalwork factory. I had to organise both projects single-handed. No help was offered or sought, apart from the weekly progress meetings with the directors.

How did I do it? How did I manage?

Well, to coin a phrase, I got by with a little help from a friend.

I have stated that the events seemed to be concentrated around the edge of where the dam used to be. As always, whenever I think I have formulated some kind of pattern to the happenings, something occurs to prove me wrong. This is what happened when the old stores were being cleared, ready for demolition.

Jane, a stock control clerk, had an office in the old stores. She worked there along with her boss, booking in the stock as it arrived into the stores and releasing stock into the assembly department in accordance with production demands. She came to me and complained that she had seen someone at the bottom of the stores the first thing every morning for the past two days. She was always the first to arrive each day, but as she unlocked the office she had seen someone in the darkness at the bottom of the stores. She had been worried about this and had asked two of the stores labourers to search the area. There was no way out of the bottom of the stores; all the main doors were by the side of the office, and that was padlocked securely. The fire doors at the bottom of the stores were locked each night by the watchman and unlocked after the work force had arrived and the building was occupied. The search found nothing and Jane had dismissed the first incident as a trick of the light, but when she saw the figure again the second day she became rather nervous. She came to me and told me of her fears. I went with Jane and searched the area. I found nothing—no way of forced entry, no evidence that someone had sneaked in during the day and spent the night there, waiting. Nothing at all to substantiate her fears. She was, however, insistent that she had seen a figure walk across the bottom of the aisle between the stacks of wooden panels. It had happened two days running the first thing in the morning as she arrived. I was sympathetic, as I could see from her reaction that she was genuinely afraid. I arranged that instead of going to her office the next morning, she would come to my office, and I would accompany her to her office and try to catch whoever it was.

The next day I arrived ten minutes earlier than normal. Jane was waiting for me. I accompanied her to her office. We stood there outside her office, watching and waiting. Nothing happened. We stood there for a good ten minutes, but there was no sign of anything or anybody. I waited with her until her boss arrived. Jane, feeling rather foolish, thanked me, and I left. I arranged that she would follow the same procedure the next day.

This arrangement lasted for the next three days. On the fourth day, as I was walking with her down the stores towards the office, I saw it; a figure crossing the bottom of the aisle between the stacks of wooden panels.

"Hey, you there!" I called. "Stop!" I was ignored.

I told Jane to go into the office and telephone for the watchman. I cautiously walked down the aisle towards where Jane and I had last seen the figure. On reaching the spot, I turned the corner. There was no one there. I walked further down the space at the end of the building. There was no one there. I returned to the office to wait for the watchman. When he arrived I explained what had occurred. He looked at me with a knowing look.

"I know what you are thinking," I said, "but search the area anyway and look for any sign of forced entry."

Nothing was found, but I arranged for the watchman to accompany Jane to her office every morning until she finally moved office in readiness for the forthcoming demolition.

At the bottom of the old stores was a room that was used to store foam rubber. The room above the foam stores also had strange things happen in it. This room had been used in the past as the upholstery section, where chair seats and cushions were made. Only two men worked up there, and they had, many times, told of doors opening on their own and other such minor happenings. I didn't take much notice of them, as such incidents were commonplace within the factory and much more dramatic incidents had absorbed my attention. The two men were finally moved into a new area, and the room was taken over as the samples room. This was where sample furniture was stored. The furniture would be transported to various exhibitions or demonstrations whenever it was required and stored in the samples room at all other times. If a customer ordered a special piece of furniture, a sample would be kept for future reference and to exhibit to other customers.

This room became the responsibility of the quality assurance manager and Alan, his assistant. Access to this room was gained by an internal staircase and an outside fire escape. The doors at the top of both flights of stairs were both kept securely locked; only the quality manager and Alan had keys.

Alan came to me and complained that someone was getting into the room and moving the furniture around. He explained that the furniture was stored in groups in order to identify which set of furniture had been supplied to which customer. Someone was mixing the pieces of furniture, and this was costing Alan a lot of time, re-sorting it and moving it back to its correct location. I accompanied him to the room.

When we arrived I saw large wardrobes and desks in a state of complete disarray. The furniture was heavy and would have needed two strong men to move it over the uneven wooden floor.

"Look at the state of this!" Alan exclaimed. "It will take me hours to sort and move this lot."

"Who would want to move it?" I asked. "Is anything missing?"

"Not that I can see," replied Alan. "Wardrobes and desks are not easy to get up and down that fire escape. No, nothing is missing; it's just been moved."

I looked at both doors, no sign of forced entry, no damage to the door and frame at all.

"Someone must have a key," I said. "The only thing I can do is have the locks changed and make sure only you and your boss have keys."

This was done. High-security locks were fitted, and the keys were issued to Alan and the quality assurance manager, with the specific instructions not to loan them to anyone and that both doors were to be kept locked unless the room was occupied, when both doors were to be unlocked in case of fire.

Two or three days later, Alan and another man happened to be in the foam stores when they heard movement from the room above, scraping, dragging noise. Someone was moving the furniture again.

"You go and stand at the fire escape," said Alan. "I'll go up the stairs. There's no other way out; we've got them this time."

Alan rushed up the stairs, only to find the door locked. He fumbled for his keys and anxiously tried to unlock the door to catch whoever it was.

He opened the door and to his surprise found the room in complete disarray once again, but there was no one in the room at all. He quickly walked over to the fire escape door. This door was also locked. He opened it and called to the man outside. "Has anyone passed you?" he asked.

"No one has passed me," was the reply. "I arrived at the bottom of this fire escape before you got up those stairs, and no one has come down this way."

"Come up and have a look at this!" called Alan.

The other man walked up the fire escape and looked at the furniture.

“Would you believe that two days ago I spent hours sorting all this into customer group, style, and model? Now look at it,” Alan complained.

“It looks a right mess,” said the other man. “We heard it being moved while we were downstairs and there was no one up here! I'm not staying here.” With that he ran down the stairs and away.

Alan looked around the room at the furniture. He wasn't certain, but the furniture looked in the same position as before he had sorted it out. After a few seconds he decided to leave things as they were. He locked the door and left.

A couple of days later, Alan again, with help, sorted the furniture into product group, style, and model. This was not an easy task with the uneven floor and the weight of the furniture. It was all to no avail, as a short time after, the furniture moved itself back into its original positions. No matter how often Alan arranged the room, someone or something moved it back again. In the end Alan decided to leave the furniture in the position it preferred. He locked the doors and only went back when absolutely necessary.

I was approached by the company directors at this point. I was asked to give up the works engineer position and take up the position of project manager. I was to be consulted on maintenance problems and asked to give technical advice, but the day-to-day running of the maintenance department was to come under the control of the factory manager.

I was asked to undertake the building and equipping of two more factories at a small town in West Yorkshire called South Kirkby. The two factories were to be built simultaneously. The larger one, some forty thousand square feet, was to start in January. The second, smaller factory, some twenty thousand square feet, to manufacture the same furniture as the other factory, was to begin construction in April.

I accepted the challenge and much of the next year was taken up with building the factories. I always tried to get back to the old factory every day. I needed to be inspired and to get the problems sorted. I could only do that at the factory.

The maintenance crew was not happy with the arrangement and said so on more than one occasion. They did not get on with the factory manager at all. They said I was their boss and, as far as they were concerned, I always would be. The two factories were completed and I returned to the old place as a technical consultant, but now I had to visit the two South Kirkby factories on a daily basis.

The next project that the directors had in mind for me was the most ambitious yet. I was to build a special factory at Normanton, in West Yorkshire, about six miles away. This factory was intended to be set up to supply the wooden panels to the three furniture-building factories.

All the machines from the original factory were to be transferred, and the complete panel production facility was to be at Normanton. Building yet again was to start in January, with completion or first production to begin on the fifth of June. This time I was to have help, as the factory manager was to assist me in the project. I did not feel this was necessary, I had done all right on my own so far, but I did not object. Unfortunately, his involvement did not last very long. . . .

There have been many works managers at Old Castle Works. The length of time that any of them held the position was between eighteen months and two years.

There were also periods lasting about six months when the company was between managers. The production seemed to carry on as normal whether they had a works manager or not.

This particular manager who held the post at the time I was planning the panel-producing factory was a pleasant-enough chap. A poor choice for the position, I thought, but I got on with him well enough.

We spent a lot of time together planning the new factory. A project such as this can take up to a year in the planning stages before a site is chosen and orders placed for the additional equipment that needs to be purchased.

One morning about a week before I was going on my summer holidays, I needed to speak to the manager; I forget what about. His office, as I have mentioned, was above the old reception area, next door to the quality assurance manager's office. Both offices had outside walls with windows overlooking the street. The paritions that separated the two had glass all the way across the top, as did the partitioning that separated the offices from the workshop. Each office had its own door, with an adjoining door between them. The works manager had a storage unit placed up against the partitioning at the end of his office and to the side. As one approached the office from the staircase, the works manager was clearly visible sitting at his desk. Through the glass at the bottom of the office he was lost from view because of the storage unit, but he could be seen again before the door was reached. A clear case of now you see him, now you don't.

I phoned him before I went up, just to make sure he was available. "Can I come and see you?" I asked. "There's a few points I need to discuss before I go on holiday next week."

"Yes," he replied." "Come on up right away if you like."

I walked up the staircase, turned right, and walked across in front of the quality assurance manager's office. I saw the works manager sitting at his desk. He was alone, writing on some papers on his desk.

He was wearing what looked like a heavy dark brown jumper with long, baggy sleeves. He had in his hand a large feather. He was writing with a quill. I lost sight of him as I passed by the storage unit.

A feather? What's he doing with a feather? I said to myself, quickly trying to think of something witty to say. When he came back into my line of vision, I stopped. He was wearing a light blue pullover and writing with a pen. I was astonished, completely astonished. The fact that I had seen him wearing a brown heavy jumper and with a quill in his hand had not surprised me until the scene changed. I had not realised what was happening until the scene had gone. I walked into his office very slowly, staring at him, my mouth wide open.

"What's the matter?" he asked, looking up from what he was doing. I couldn't reply; I was totally speechless.

"What's wrong?" he asked.

"Sorry," I said, finding my voice. "I'll have to come back later."

I went back to my office in a daze, thinking about what I had seen. Brian, the maintenance supervisor, who also had a desk in the same office, came in and sat down.

"What's the matter with you?" he asked.

"Brian," I said, "I know this sounds crazy, but I have just seen the works manager dressed as a monk and writing with a quill."

Brian was as used to hearing strange stories as I was. "Do you want to tell me the whole story?"

"I think I had better," I replied, and I relayed the whole event to him.

"Why are you so worried about it?" he asked when I had finished. "You've seen and experienced stranger things than that."

"True," I replied, "but I have never seen it actually change someone's appearance before. I don't like it. I wonder if I should tell him."

"You must be joking!" Brian exclaimed. "What will that achieve? He will only think you are mad, or if he believes you, he will worry about it."

We discussed it further but agreed there was nothing to be done.

This time I told my wife what I had seen. She already knew of some of the happenings and about Charlie. There are not many things I keep from her. She was as worried about it as I was, but what could we do?

My wife, our son, and I went away on holiday as arranged for two weeks beginning the following Saturday. We had a really good time—sea, sun, sand, and good food. My wife and I forgot all about Charlie; we just enjoyed ourselves.

We returned home two weeks later on the Saturday afternoon. As usual there was a pile of letters behind the front door, letters that had been delivered whilst we had been on holiday.

When we had unloaded the car, I sat down to go through the mail. I was surprised to find a letter from the factory. I opened it and found it was from one of the directors of the company. This is what I read:

Dear Peter,

It is my unfortunate task to inform you that the works manager has suffered a massive brain hemorrhage and is not expected to survive. It happened while he was driving home and he is in hospital undergoing a series of operations.

I thought it best to inform you of this before you returned to work on Monday morning. I am sure you join me in wishing him well.

Yours sincerely,

I showed the letter to my wife.

"Isn't that the man you saw dressed in the monk's habit?" she asked.

"Yes, it is," I replied. "Do you think it was a warning?"

"I don't want to think about it," she replied. "It's frightening." It was worrying; that was for sure.

Was it a warning? Should I have told him? The answers to these questions I will never know.

Fortunately, he did survive, but he suffered terrible brain damage and his recovery will take many years.

I have not mentioned him by name for obvious reasons. He is alive and still recovering, and I wish him well.

The Normanton project continued and was successfully completed. I had to organise everything myself, since the works manager was no longer with us. The factory was built, all services were installed, and the machines were transferred. Many new machines were also purchased and installed; this meant fewer people were needed to operate them.

Many redundancies came about with the opening of the Normanton factory. Included in those redundancies was the maintenance crew. The two original watchmen had retired three years before and been replaced by two younger men. One of the new watchmen was made redundant with the others. The painter was made redundant, as were two of my labourers. The maintenance supervisor and one electrician were transferred to the new factory, and the two fitters were offered work if they accepted their redundancies and became self-employed. This offer was extended to the painter. All three accepted, and I still provide work for them all.

This left Graham, the electrician and the joiner. Both were retained at the factory.

The next task I had to fulfil was the demolition of the rest of the old factory. Most of the ground floor had been vacated, but I had to provide additional office space in the new building, and the cabinet shop also had to be relocated in there. With much organising and moving things about, this was achieved. I also had to provide to all sections of the site that were not included in the demolition programme all electric supplies, heating, water, telephones, data cables, and fire alarm systems. All services ran through the old factory. They had to be rerouted to allow the old building to be demolished.

The amount of organising and reorganising of that operation is difficult to describe due to its complexity, and as usual, I was on my own. No help in organising or designing such a complex operation was available from anyone, but as always, I had Charlie.

I would sit in my office and puzzle over how a certain thing could be done, and then, as though a light had been turned on in my head, the answer was there.

The whole of the old building had to be pulled down, with the exception of the boiler house and the flat-panel building. All the rest had to go.

I wondered what reacton I would get from my supernatural friend—well, not from Charlie, who had helped to organise everything, but how many other forces were there, and would they approve? . . .

During the demolition some strange things happened, things that were bizarre and very difficult to believe. I am reluctant to include them in this book for fear that they may discredit the rest of the events that happened over the years. I have been persuaded to include them, but if the reader finds them too much like something out of a low-budget horror film, then I can only give my assurance that the events did happen. I would also like to say that I would not have believed them myself if I had not witnessed them personally.

Before the actual dismantling of the building took place I had to organise the removal of part of the heating system. The steam was to be distributed around the site to the parts of the building that were to remain intact. This was to be done by running the pipe work underground, below the old factory floor. To do this trenches had to be dug inside the factory, after the removal of the machinery, and pipe work to take the steam laid in the trenches together with ducts to accommodate electric cables, data and telephone cables, and water pipes.

The two fitters who had been made redundant had become self-employed, and I engaged them to work on rerouting the heating pipes from above ground level to below ground level.

The factory had been completely emptied of all machinery and of all usable material. The fitters needed a place to have their tea break and also to have their lunch. They chose the old electricians' workshop as this was a small room that was away from the dirt and dust created by the removal of the overhead pipe work. The room had been completely emptied with the exception of three or four chairs and a small oil drum that was used as a table by placing a square of plywood on the top of it. The room also had a door that could be closed to keep out the dirt caused by the demolition. The door was fitted with a lock that had not been used for years. The key to the door had been lost a long time ago, but the fitters kept it closed to keep their tools as safe as was reasonably practicable.

On this particular day the two fitters, Gary and Brian, were sitting having their lunch at about twelve-thirty in the afternoon. They had both finished eating and had their feet up on the makeshift table when the door of the room suddenly slammed shut. Gary and Brian looked at each other.

"Who did that?" asked Gary.

"Don't ask me," replied Brian. "Must have been the wind."

"Wind, what wind?" asked Gary. "We are in the heart of the factory. The wind can't get to here. Someone must have closed it."

"There's no one else in the building," said Brian.

"No one's supposed to be in the building, you mean," replied Gary. "Doors don't close on their own."

"Oh, leave it," said Brian. "So the door closed; so what?"

They both settled back down to enjoy what was left of their lunch break before starting work again at one o'clock.

"Come on," said Gary in a few minutes, as he looked at his watch. "We had better make a move."

They both got up, tidying the sandwich papers away. They picked up their tools and walked to the door.

"This door's stuck," said Brian as he tried to open the door.

"Give it a push," said Gary. "It'll go."

Brian pushed harder. "It won't move. It's stuck good and proper."

"Come out of the way," snapped Gary. "You've lost all your strength."

Gary put his tools down and tried to open the door. He took hold of the handle and slammed his shoulder against the door. The door did not move.

"It's not stuck," said Gary. "It's locked."

"Locked?" repeated Brian. "How can it be locked? There isn't a key; that lock hasn't been used in years."

"Well, it's locked now," said Gary angrily. "How the hell are we going to get out of here now?"

They looked around the room. It was a solidly built room, the walls made of brick, and it had a small window that led out onto the alleyway between the old factory and the new building. This window had been fitted with a strong wire mesh to prevent anyone from gaining entry to the factory from outside. There was no way out through there.

"We'll have to shout for help," said Brian.

"Save your breath," said Gary. "You said yourself that there is no one else in the building. Who's going to hear us?"

"If there's no one in the building, who locked the door?" asked Brian.

"Good point," agreed Gary. "Whoever it is, they are probably standing at the other side of the door, laughing. Put your ear to the door and see if you can hear anything."

Brian put his ear to the wooden door and listened. Nothing, not a sound, could he hear. "No, I can't hear a thing."

"Let me have a try," said Gary. He put his ear to the door, but nothing could be heard.

Gary, losing his patience, banged with his fist on the door. "Whoever is there, open this door!" he shouted.

He listened again; only silence could be heard.

"There's no one there," he said. "We are locked in and there is no one to let us out."

"What do we do now?" asked Brian. "We will be in here forever, prisoners, until they knock the roof in on top of us."

"Well, I'm not sitting around waiting for that to happen," said Gary. "I am getting out of here, even if I have to take a wall down to do it."

"The door is the weakest point," said Brian. "We will have to smash it down."

"Just what I was thinking," said Gary. "What have you got in the way of tools?"

Brian looked in his toolbox. "A large screwdriver will help," he said as he took it from the box.

"Good," said Gary. "And I've got a hammer."

They set to work cutting their way through the solid wooden door. They concentrated on the wood around the lock and also the door frame, banging and hammering the wood until the area around the lock was weakened sufficiently for the door to be kicked open.

After about an hour of chiselling and hammering, they stood back. Standing side by side, they both kicked the door at the same time. It did not move. They set to work again at the wood around the lock. They cut all the way through the door and then hit the area of the lock with the hammer continually until the lock itself finally fell out of the woodwork and landed on the other side of the door.

"At last," said Gary. "Come on; let's get out of here."

He pushed the door, but still it refused to open.

"What's going on?" he said. "I don't like this. The lock has been removed, but the door still will not open; it must be screwed shut."

"How could someone have done that, while we were having our sandwiches?" asked Brian.

"I don't know," replied Gary, "but we are not going to get out of here as easily as we thought. We will have to take the whole door and frame down in order to get out."

"That will take forever," said Brian.

"Yes," agreed Gary. "We had better get on with it."

The pair started hammering at the door frame, at the brickwork, the only way they could think of to get out of the room.

While all this was going on, I was sat in my office, taking phone calls and generally organising the demolition programme. I had a temporary office, built in the corner of the old flat-panel department; it was from there that I controlled everything and made my plans for the next stages of the work.

Better go and check on how the fitters are doing, I thought to myself. I had not seen them since this morning, but they were good workers, so I did not have to stand over them every minute of the day.

I walked downstairs to the place where the fitters should have been working. Not a sign of them. Puzzled, I started to look for them. I could hear the sounds of hammering in the distance, coming from somewhere in the heart of the factory. I followed the noises. The sounds of hammering led me to the old fitting shop and to the abandoned electricians' department. I walked in and I could see the door to the room was closed and the lock from the door had been cut away. It was lying on the floor just in front of the door. I could see through the hole in the door some movement and hear the sounds of hammering on the brickwork around the door frame.

"What on earth are you doing?" I shouted through the door.

The hammering stopped.

"Is someone there?" a voice came from the inside.

"Yes, it's me," I replied. "What on earth are you doing?"

"We are locked in; we've been trying to get out since lunchtime."

"What do you mean, locked in?" I asked. "The lock isn't even on the door."

"I know. It must be nailed shut. Can you see from that side?"

I looked at the door; there were no nails or screws showing. "Are you having me on or what?" I asked.

I took hold of the door by putting my hand through the hole where the lock had been and pulled the door open. "This door isn't locked at all," I said.

As I opened the door I was met by two wide-eyed, open-mouthed fitters.

"That door was locked," they both said in harmony. "We have been trying to get out for an hour and a half."

"Well, it isn't locked now," I snapped. "Come on; get on with that pipe work. I've got a schedule to keep, and we have lost nearly half a day."

With that I walked back to my office. Both the fitters came to see me at the end of the day and told me that the door certainly had been locked and that they were trying to get out. As I could not think of any good reason for them to behave as they did and why they should be hammering at the door and frame, I reluctantly agreed to believe their story.

*   *   *

Another event that happened while the building was being dismantled is probably the most unbelievable of them all, but it happened just the same. It could be that the building itself had been there for so long that it had been taken over by the spirits and had become part of them, an extension to their bodiless forms, the only material connection between their world and this one. Perhaps it was the building itself that was the problem. I had set in motion the process of destroying it. This next event could be symbolic of this, a sign, perhaps, to try to show me that I was destroying part of them, that I was killing something that was alive and, through my ignorance, ripping out the very heart of their existence, but judge for yourselves.

The demolition was well under way. The firm of contractors had actually paid the company for the job of dismantling the building, and they had set about trying to salvage as much reusable material as they could. This was necessary in order to recoup their investment and make as much profit as possible. Some of the resaleable items were the floorboards and the large wooden beams that formed the upper floor. These were removed with great care and attention. They were taken up by hand and loaded onto lorries for removal from the site. One thing that hampered this operation was the electric cables that were run in metal conduits and fastened to the underside of the large wooden beams. The conduits ran along the roof of the ground floor and down the walls to where the machines had been positioned. Obviously, these cables and conduits had to be removed before the beams could be taken down. The electricians who were employed by the demolition company did this by removing the conduits from the wall, unscrewing them from the connecting piece fastened to the beams, and pulling them from their positions, leaving the heavy-duty cables hanging down the wall. They would then cut the cables as close to the wooden beam as possible. This allowed the beams to be removed, and the remaining section of the cable was taken from the beam once it was at ground level. I was watching the operation of removing the cables from the conduits, even though I probably should not have been there, as I had handed all responsibility for the site over to the demolition company. This is what happened. . . .

"This is a nasty, dirty job," I said to Bob, the electrician employed by the demolition company.

"You're right there," he replied. "This dust gets everywhere. You expect dust and dirt on this sort of work, but with this being an old woodworking factory, the dust is far worse than anything I have experienced before."

"Haven't you got a dust mask?" I asked.

"Yes," he replied, "but I can't work with that thing on; it makes me too hot and it blocks up very easily."

"You should wear it; anything's better than breathing this dust all day long."

"I do wear it when the dust gets really bad, but just now, while I'm just removing cables, it's not too bad."

We chatted like this while I watched him unscrew the saddles holding the large-diameter conduit to the wall. When he had done this he took a pipe wrench and unscrewed the conduit from the jointing piece that was anchored to the wooden joists in the ceiling. He then pulled the tube from the electric cables, leaving them hanging down the wall.

He fetched a pair of stepladders and, placing them under the hanging cables, climbed the steps, a large pair of wire cutters in his hand. There were four cables in all, one for each of the three-phase supply and a neutral. Snip, snip, snip, snip, went the wire cutters as he cut through the cables one by one, letting them fall to the floor. Suddenly there was blood everywhere; it was splattered on the wall, and Bob was covered in it.

"I must have cut myself!" shouted Bob as he quickly came down the stepladder. He held his hands out, dropping the wire cutters to the floor.

I quickly examined his hands. "I don't see a cut," I said, "but your hands are so dirty I can't see anything. Go and get them washed, and then I will take you to the hospital, if that's what is needed. I'll wait for you here."

He rushed off in the direction of the new part of the factory. That was the only place where there were washing facilities, as the water had been cut off to this old part of the factory. I would have gone with him, but I knew he was not injured. I had seen where the blood had come from. Not from him—it was coming from the cables, at least from one of the cables. One of the solid copper cables was bleeding.

Shocked but not afraid, I looked up at the cable. I was well past being afraid of such things by now. I stared up at the cable. Was I mistaken? Could it have been Bob who was cut after all?

No mistake. I watched as the blood went drip, drip, drip onto the floor, making an ever-increasing puddle as it splashed onto the concrete floor.

"Sorry, Charlie," I said. "I hope that didn't hurt too much."

There was no reply—of course there was no reply; we never had communicated by sound. Not from Charlie to me anyway.

What was I to do? I could not let Bob know that such things happened around here. He would probably walk off the job and report it to the newspapers or something. I had to work and think quickly.

I got a piece of rag and went up the stepladder. I looked closely at the cables; the blood was only coming from one of them. It had stopped dripping by now and formed a pear-shaped blob on the end of the cable. I tied the end in a tight knot, as tight as I could get with a thick copper cable, and wiped the end to remove any sign that the blood had come from the copper wire. I looked closely at the end, watching for any sign that it was still bleeding. No, the bleeding had stopped. I tried to clean the blood off the white emulsion–painted walls. It would not come off. I went down the ladder and took a handful of dust and dirt and returned to the wall. I rubbed the dirt onto the wall in an effort to disguise the red marks. This was better than nothing, but it did not hide very much. I did the same with the blood on the floor. I piled dust and dirt onto it and rubbed hard with the sole of my shoe. I had just finished that when Bob came back.

"I'm not cut at all," said Bob. "Where did that blood come from?"

"It wasn't blood," I laughed, lying through my teeth. "It was the red PVC insulation on the cable. Some thinners or something must have got into the conduit and rotted the insulation, making it wet and liquid. It must have run down the cable when you removed the metal conduit."

"If that's true," said Bob, "why only the red cable? What about the blue and the yellow or even the black?"

"I can't explain that," I replied. "But don't worry about it. You're not hurt; that's the main thing."

I put my hand on his shoulder and led him away from the area, doing my best to change the subject. He stopped occasionally to look back at the spot, but I managed to get his mind onto something more important, like the latest cricket scores and what was on television that evening. It worked, but I never saw Bob again after that day. I think he asked to be transferred to another job. I wonder what excuse he gave.

It was almost seven o'clock in the evening. The cleaners, Shirley and Trish, were standing by the clock waiting to clock out after finishing their cleaning duty. It was an arduous task, trying to keep the offices clean with all the demolition work going on. Dust was brought in on people's shoes, and the dirt seemed to get everywhere.

This new building was the only part of the factory that was occupied. The old building was being demolished, but they were only stripping the old building of all salvageable material. Heavy cables, pipe work, beams, floorboards, and that type of thing were been ripped out first. The dust created by this activity was a major problem. This was, after all, a woodworking factory that had been used as such since 1890, and the buildings, or some of them, had even been in use before that date.

A new upper-floor office suite had been built in order to accommodate all the people left from the old part of the factory after the redundancies. The extra office space that needed cleaning had put more strain on the cleaning ladies. More hours had been offered, but both the ladies had children and needed to be home at a reasonable hour. Occasionally they would work late, but they had to make arrangements beforehand and needed a couple of days' notice before they could. Trish also worked three hours in the mornings, from 9:00 A.M. until 12 noon. Shirley only worked the three hours in the evenings.

There was only one watchman now; he was on permanent days. He left at 6:00 P.M., so the cleaners had the added responsibility of locking the new building before they left for home.

To my knowledge, they had not been told of any strange happenings. I had not told them and I had given instructions to my people not to tell them. They would probably give up the job if they were told the truth. They hadn't been with us very long, and they were good workers. Besides, there had been no events reported in the new building, so there was nothing to tell.

"Is that clock right?" asked Shirley.

"Of course it is," replied Trish. "Doesn't a minute seem a long time?"

"This place gives me the creeps," said Shirley. "I'm always glad to get out of here."

"Yes, I know what you mean," said Trish. "It seems different in the daytime. It's probably because it's such a high building and it normally has a lot of noise and people moving about."

"Come on, clock," said Shirley, giving it a knock.

"Don't do that!" cried Trish. "You'll break it. We'll have to do more hours."

"What? And stop here even later?" exclaimed Shirley. "Not likely."

"It's alright for you," said Trish, "but they get on to me in the morning. 'Why haven't you cleaned this? Why haven't you done that?' I tell them there isn't time. We'll have to stop and give it a good going-over."

"I'll give this clock a good going-over if it doesn't hurry up!" cried Shirley, who was not really listening.

Just then the clock hand moved to seven o'clock.

"At last," said Shirley as she quickly put her clock card in, and the time-piece printed the time on it.

Trish did the same and they were both placing their cards in the rack when they heard a noise at the top end of the building.

"What was that?" asked Trish.

The sound was a low rumbling noise.

"I don't know," replied Shirley.

They both stopped and listened.

"It must have been a lorry going past," said Trish.

"That noise came from inside," said Shirley. "I'm sure it did."

They both cautiously started to walk down the long building towards the door. It was the only way out onto the roadway, unless they went through the old building, but they were not about to do that. They had to walk in the direction the noise had come from. The aisle they walked down was by the side of a high block-work wall. This aisle was the only part of the building that was illuminated.

"Do you think someone has come in?" asked Shirley.

"No, they can't get in. Everywhere is locked," replied Trish.

"Is anyone there?' shouted Shirley.

They both stopped and listened.

"There's no one there," said Trish. "We're being stupid; come on."

They quickened their pace, holding onto each other's arm. The noise started again, only louder this time—a low rumbling noise, almost like a metal-wheeled trolley was being pulled over concrete.

They stopped, not daring to move.

"It's behind the wall," said Trish.

As she spoke, the rumbling noise grew louder still. It started from the far end of the wall but seemed to come from a point some eight feet from the ground. The pair just stood there motionless, petrified.

The noise moved quickly down the length of the wall, still maintaining its height from the floor. It ran down the other side of the wall. As it passed by the cleaning ladies, who were by now crouching down, covering their heads, the floor began to vibrate, shaking with the noise. It quickly passed the spot where they were crouching and travelled on down the wall. The noise suddenly stopped as it came to the end of the wall. A brief second of silence, then a crash, a loud crash, as a force hit the roller shutter door. The noise had left the wall and travelled the fifteen-metre gap before hitting one of the loading bay doors.

"Come on," said Trish. "Run." She had set off running a few paces when she realised Shirley was not with her. She stopped, quickly looked back, and saw Shirley still crouched down.

"I can't," she cried, still in the same position.

Trish ran back and grabbed her arm. "Come on," said Trish as she pulled Shirley to her feet and half-dragged her towards the door. Shirley resisted at first and then stated running with Trish, keeping one hand behind her as she ran. They quickly ran out of the building after fumbling with the lock on the door and over to Trish's car in the car park.

"Let me in the back," said Shirley.

"Why in the back?" asked Trish.

"Don't argue; please let me in the back," sobbed Shirley, almost in tears.

"All right," said Trish.

They both got in and quickly drove off. They didn't speak for a few minutes.

"What do you think it was?" asked Trish.

"I don't know and I don't want to talk about it," snapped Shirley.

They stayed silent for a few more minutes as Trish drove through the town centre.

"Have you got a plastic bag or something?" asked Shirley.

"What for?" asked Trish.

"Don't ask," replied Shirley. "Have you?"

"There's a carrier bag in the glove box," replied Trish, puzzled.

Shirley reached over from the back of the car and took the plastic carrier bag from the glove box. "Will you stop in a side street when we're out of the town centre?"

"What for?" asked Trish. "I want to get home after an ordeal like that."

"I've had an accident, if you must know!" cried Shirley.

"You mean you have—"

"Yes," replied Shirley and she burst into tears.

Trish pulled over at the first opportunity. Shirley removed her soiled underwear and wrapped it in the plastic carrier bag, and they both drove home.

Trish came to see me as soon as she arrived the next morning. She asked me if Shirley and she could come and speak to me at ten o'clock that morning. I asked why.

"I'd rather not say until Shirley gets here," she said.

"Fine, I'll see you both at ten."

At ten o'clock they both came into my office. Shirley had made a special journey just to see me.

I asked what the problem was, and they told me of their previous night's experience, although their description of Shirley's accident was more colourful and detailed than I have described. They refused to stay in the factory alone again and used Shirley's accident as proof that they had given an accurate account of what had happened. I agreed to change the watchman's hours so he was with them until they left the factory, whatever the time happened to be. I had been unhappy that the cleaners had to carry the responsibility for security and was not sorry that I was forced to make alternative arrangements. This satisfied the cleaners and they went away happier than when they arrived.

This was the first report of any strange events that I had received from the new building. In fact, it was the first report of anything from that part of the site.

Had the forces found a new home or had other forces been disturbed by the demolition?

Chapter 9

The cleaning ladies told everyone about what they had experienced. The shop floor workers just made jokes about it, but the office workers, who were mostly young people, new to the factory, became very interested. Pretty soon everyone was hearing things and seeing things. I was bombarded with sightings and all sorts of strange events. It only needed a chair to fall over or a paper to move, probably from a draught from an open window, for it to be a ghost or something.

It was almost mass hysteria. No one on the office side would work late or come early or be in the building alone at any time. I dismissed almost all their stories as exaggerations or even downright lies. I was too experienced by now to be taken in by what clearly were made-up stories. Not one event was substantiated, all the events happened to only one person at any time, and none of the events fitted into the overall picture that I had built up over the period of time that I had been living with these things. It also made matters worse if I appeared to believed them. "If Peter Jackson believed it, then it must be true," was the general opinion. I did not give any indication that I knew that something was present on the site. The offices would have been evacuated in five minutes flat if I had.

This next story, which I have put in for good measure, was one of those that came forward during that brief time when everyone was seeing ghosts. It is unsubstantiated and there were no witnesses, but I have included it because it came from an older shop floor worker, not a silly, hysterical teenage girl office worker, and because he really was scared enough to leave the factory, risking his job and losing money in the bargain. I have also included it because of its originality.

It had been a long, hard day in the assembly area. An order for dispatch had to go out the following morning. They were late in completing assembly, so the supervisor had asked for volunteers to work late to complete the job. Dave and five other cabinetmakers had agreed to work late that night. The supervisor also stopped late to make sure the work was done.

It was wintertime and the dark nights were upon us. With only six people working, most of the lights in the factory had been turned off. The stores area, which is adjacent to the assembly area, is a high building with pallet racking in rows forming alleyways. The panels and parts were stored in the racking, each rack labelled with the part number.

The lights in the stores had been turned off, and the quietness of the area seemed overpowering.

Dave, a level-headed, down-to-earth sort of chap, was working away when he noticed one of the component parts of the desk he was building was damaged. He called the supervisor over.

"What do you want me to do about this?" Dave asked.

"Scrap it," was the reply. "Go to the stores and get another. I'll sort the paperwork in the morning."

Dave removed the faulty panel and put it to one side. He obtained the part number and went to the stores to try to locate the correct rack. Not being that familiar with the stores layout, he had to walk the alleyways looking for the part. He switched some of the lights on in order to see the labelled racks and walked slowly down the rows looking for the replacement part, walking first down one row and then down the next, looking at the racks all the time.

Suddenly something touched the back of his head, something gentle and soft. He stopped, looked up; there was nothing there. He was totally alone, and not a sound could be heard. He looked on the floor. Had something fallen on him from the high racks? He could find nothing, no evidence of anything at all.

What was that? he said to himself as he put his hand on his head where he had felt something or someone touch him. *Imagination,* he thought to himself, but a chill ran down his spine. Quickening his pace, he started looking more intensely for the part he required.

At last he found the rack. There it was, one shelf up from hand height.

Damn it, he thought. *I need a ladder, Blow that; I'll climb up the racks.*

Slowly he climbed about five feet from the ground to the level he required. He looked into the rack in the half-light, pushing his head into the rack space.

Without warning, a hand shot out from the shadows and stroked his face.

"AHHH!" he cried and fell backwards. He landed on the hard concrete floor, which winded him for a second. He got up and walked backwards away from the rack.

"Who's there?" he cried, thinking it was one of the lads, messing about. "Come on; who's there?"

There was no response. He walked cautiously backwards, his eyes fixed on the rack. Silence filled the stores once again. Bump, he came to a sudden halt as he walked into the racks at the back of him. He stopped, half-turned, when a hand came out of that rack and reached for his face. Panic hit him and he started to run the fifty metres or so down the alleyway between the racks. Hands came out from everywhere, reaching, touching, stroking his head and face. Running through a tunnel of hands, he screamed and yelled as he went.

His workmates, hearing him, stopped working and turned to see what was wrong. They saw Dave, white with fright, come running from the stores. He did not stop to talk to anyone. He ran past his bench, leaving his coat and sandwich box where they were, straight out of the building, and into his car and drove off at high speed into the night.

His workmates and the supervisor looked on in amazement. When they had recovered somewhat they ventured, as a group, to the entrance of the stores. They switched on all the lights and looked carefully round the area. Everything seemed normal, no evidence of anything unusual.

What did Dave see to make him behave like that? they wondered.

"Back to work!" shouted the supervisor. "I'll see Dave in the morning."

The next day Dave arrived but would not speak to anyone or answer any questions his workmates asked him. The supervisor called him into the office. Having heard what Dave had to say, he telephoned me and asked if I could come to his office and listen to Dave's story. This I did and what I heard is what I have written here.

Speaking to the cabinet shop manager about the incident later, I told him of my suspicions that the story was mostly fiction or a great exaggeraton of what actually did happen.

He seemed surprised. "Why don't you believe the total story?" he asked.

"It doesn't fit with the other reports; it seems to be one on its own, no witnesses, and different from anything I have been told before in all the years I've been here," I replied.

"What is so different?" he asked.

"The actual seeing of hands and arms. Yes, we have had lots of cases where people, including myself, have felt something touch them on their face or head and even on the back of their hand, but no one has ever seen the hands and arms as Dave described."

"What?" he cried. "They may not have seen them recently, but let me tell you, when I was an apprentice, just about everyone was talking about seeing hands and arms reaching for and touching your face or head."

"I haven't heard about that," I replied. "When was this?"

"Back in the late fifties," he replied, "and something happened to me at that time and let me tell you, as a young lad of fifteen, it frightened me to death. I have never forgotten the experience and I now believe all the stories, and if Dave said that is what happened, then that's what happened."

"I would like to hear of your experience from all those years ago; it may help me to believe Dave's story."

"Well, sit down and I will tell you."

I sat in the chair opposite his desk, and Dennis relayed the story to me. . . .

"Has that old bloke been telling you about the ghostly arms?" said young Dennis to one of his mates as he and a gang of three other youths had a quick smoke in the backyard of the factory. It was 1959 and the lads had only left school three months ago. This was their first job, and the old hands were always teasing them and telling them stories. They had learned by now not to take what was said as the whole truth. They had had many tricks played on them and did not know who was serious and who was not. The result was that they treated everything that was told to them with suspicion.

"Yes," said one of the lads, taking the cigarette from his mouth. "Silly old fool, does he think we are going to fall for a story like that? He must think we are thick or something."

"I know," said Dennis. "I would like to teach him a lesson for trying to scare the living daylights out of us, as if he could."

"What? Give him a taste of his own medicine?"

"That's exactly what I mean," replied Dennis. "I'll think of something, but we had better get back inside before the foreman misses us. I'll have a plan by tomorrow."

With that the four lads crept back inside the factory and continued with their work.

The next day the four lads met up again for their usual quick smoke and to formulate their plan.

"Well, have you thought of something?" one of the lads asked Dennis.

"Yes," Dennis replied, "and it's a good one. This will scare him out of his stupid mind."

"Serves him right," laughed one of the lads. "Let's hear it then."

"Hear what?"

"The plan, the plan."

"Oh, right," said Dennis. "Well, you know he works over every night?"

"Yes," said the lads together.

"When everyone has gone, he always goes and has a cup of tea and a read of the paper at the back of that pile of mattresses over by the loading bay."

"Does he?" they all replied.

"Yes. He thinks no one knows, but it's common knowledge among the cabinet makers."

"Well, what of it?" asked one of the lads.

"I am going to pretend to go home, but I will climb on top of the mattresses and wait. When he comes for his read, I will reach over and touch the top of his stupid bald head with my hand. I will get some cold water and keep my hand in it until he comes along, and then I will touch his head and his face with a cold, wet, clammy hand. He'll probably have a heart attack."

"We love it! We love it!" laughed the other lads. "Can we stay and watch?"

"No," replied Dennis. "It would only need one of you to sneeze or something to give the game away. Wait for me at the top of the street, it should only take twenty minutes or so, and I will tell you what happens."

"We'll miss all the fun."

"I'll tell you all about it," replied Dennis, "and besides, the important thing is that we give that old codger a taste of his own medicine."

Dennis finally got the other lads to agree, and they went back to work.

Dennis could not wait for finishing time to come around. He kept looking at the old clock on the wall; it moved so slowly. He had difficulty in finding a container suitable for the water. He thought it was important for his hand to be as cold and wet as possible when he touched the old man's head. Dennis finally came up with the idea of getting some rag, soaking it in water, and wrapping it around his hand and wrist. This would have the desired effect and with no risk of spillage.

This is exactly what he did. Just before finishing time, he went to the washroom, soaked a length of rag in cold water, and wrapped it around his lower arm and hand. He put his coat over the rag and went to clock out as usual. He hung around until he was last in line, trying to behave normally. As he passed the loading bay, he quickly looked around to see if anyone was watching, then slipped, unseen, behind the pile of mattresses. The mattresses were stacked about six feet high. He had difficulty climbing on to the top of them, but finally he managed it. He lay face-down on the mattresses and took his wet arm out of his jacket and lay there waiting.

As he expected, after about five minutes, the lights went out. He moved to the edge of the mattresses and looked over. *Got to get in the correct position,* he thought to himself. He saw the wooden box that the old man used as a seat for his nightly reading sessions. *How does he read in this half-light?* Dennis wondered as he lay there. Only the lights needed to illuminate the walkway were left on in that area, and Dennis was beginning to feel a little uncomfortable, alone in the loading bay in the dark. *What if the stories are true?* he thought to himself as he lay there. He suddenly went cold. "I hope he hurries up," he whispered to himself. "This wet arm is making me feel very cold."

He was getting restless, the feeling of uneasiness getting more intense.

"At last," he said to himself as the old man came walking along to take his usual break before starting his overtime work.

The old man sat down on the wooden box, took out his vacuum flask, and poured himself a cup of tea. Placing the cup on the floor, he took out of his pocket a folded-up newspaper and a torch. He took a sip of his tea. Placing the cup back onto the floor, he proceeded to read the newspaper by the light of his pocket torch.

Dennis, meanwhile, kept very still, waiting for the most opportune moment to play his trick. He needed the right moment for the best effect. He still had this uneasy feeling, although the presence of the old man made him feel a little better.

After about ten minutes the old man put his paper down, switched off his torch, and leaned back onto the mattresses. He closed his eyes.

"He's going to have a snooze," whispered Dennis to himself. "This is it."

This was the moment Dennis had been waiting for. He slowly removed the rag from his hand, shifted his body sideways, and put his hand over the side just above the old man's head. He pulled his head back out of sight.

The old man felt the movement through the matresses and turned and looked up just as Dennis put his cold, clammy hand straight onto the old man's face.

The old man saw this long, thin arm reaching and touching his head and face. He let out an earsplitting scream and shot off as fast as his legs could carry him.

Dennis doubled up with laughter. "That'll teach the old sod to make up stories," he said to himself as he laughed uncontrollably.

His laughter was soon cut short. Something grabbed him by the shirt collar and the seat of his pants and lifted him three feet into the air. He was held there for two or three seconds. What was happening? He tried to cry out. Either the shock had rendered him speechless or the pressure of his collar on his throat stopped him, but he could not make any sound at all. Legs and arms kicking, struggling and grabbing at fresh air, he just hung there and then he dropped. He bounced off the mattresses and landed with a crash on the top of the wooden box. Dennis never felt a thing. In a mixture of shock, fear, and total panic he picked himself up and ran, like he had never run before—out of the factory, up the street, and straight past the lads who were waiting.

"What happened?" the lads called as Dennis flew past them. "Stop! What's going on?"

He did not stop until he was totally exhausted. Then he sat and waited for the other lads to catch up with him.

When they arrived, Dennis told them what had happened, and never again did they doubt any of the stories that the old factory hands told them.

"Is that all true?" I asked when Dennis had finished telling the story. "It sounds a little far-fetched to me."

"It is all absolutely true," he replied. "The only good thing to come out of it was that it stopped the old man from sneaking off and having a read and a sleep during overtime work."

* * *

The period of time in which everyone was seeing ghosts and the like lasted until the old building was completely demolished. The management of the factory made an effort to play down the stories. They could not permit their employees to be subjected to daily episodes that frightened the more impressionable, to the great delight of the office bullies.

The management could not exactly ban the stories, but they did have words with anyone who took great delight in spreading rumours and gossip over such events, true or not. News of lots of sightings and actual events may have been lost during this period, as people were discouraged from speaking about them, even to me.

It was about this time that I decided to start writing down these stories, to save them for posterity and so the real events could be separated from the fiction. After all, the factory was no longer in existence and, apart from the cleaners' story, I did not know for certain that there would be any more to write about. How wrong I was. The events of the past few years should have told me that the power that exists on this land is eternal and buildings come and buildings go, but the power goes on. . . .

Something stirred in the darkness outside Alan's office, a scraping, shifting noise, almost as though someone was dragging a wood pallet across the concrete floor. Alan, now the quality manager, had a temporary office next door to mine, in the old flat-panel department. The two offices had been built to accommodate Alan and me while the demolition was in progress and until further office accommodation was provided after the site had been cleared and the new buildings had been erected. There were plans to turn the old flat-panel department into a photographic studio for use by the sales department to photograph the furniture for publication in their sales literature and brochures. These plans had to wait until the demolition was over and all the dirt and dust had been removed. In the meantime, the area was used to store the surplus piece parts that the factory only needed on an occasional basis.

It was five-thirty on a winter evening when Alan, working in his office, heard the strange scraping, shuffling noise. He was aware of the unexplainable events that were common occurrences in the old factory. He was the person who had seen the footprints in the dust many years before. He worked as a cabinetmaker in those days and had worked his way up to become the quality manager, taking over the job from the manager who had experienced the banging wall episode two years before.

Nervous but not afraid, Alan walked to his office door, opened it, and peered out into the darkness. All the lights in the area had been turned off, and the stillness of the building did nothing to inspire his confidence.

"Who's there?" he called nervously, his voice with a slight tremor as he shouted into the blackness. The noise stopped. In fact, the noise had stopped the moment Alan opened the office door. He listened intensely for any sound or any indication at all that someone was out there, in the darkness. There was no response. He walked two paces out from his office and peered once again into the large silent area, the light from his office doorway casting long black shadows across the concrete floor.

"Is someone there?" he called again. There was no response, only the distant noise of traffic from the main road, some two hundred metres away, along Black Walk.

"I must be hearing things," he said to himself as he returned to his office to complete his paperwork.

He walked into his office and closed the door. Sitting down, he was about to continue with his work when the noise occurred again. "There is someone out there," he said to himself as he quickly got up from his chair. He was getting angry now. Someone was making a fool of him, and he was not about to tolerate that.

The noise ceased the moment the office door opened. Alan walked straight out into the darkness to the door on the outside wall. The light switches were located by the door. Alan was going to investigate the cause of the noise thoroughly. As he switched on the lights, his eyes were momentarily dazzled by the brightness. He thought he saw something move by the side of his office. "Who is it? What do you want?" he asked, his voice now stern and full of confidence. He felt that he was now in charge of the situation; he could see and this gave him a feeling of security. Walking over to where he had seen movement, he started looking around the pallets and stacks of panels stored in a disorderly manner across the floor. He found nothing, no one, no sign at all of whatever he had heard, whatever had been making the scraping sound. After a few minutes' searching, feeling puzzled and frustrated, Alan returned to the outside door and turned off the main lights. The light from his office again made long shadows across the concrete floor.

No sooner had Alan returned to his office than the noise started again. He had not closed the door this time, as though he had expected to hear it. He quickly left his office and was making for the light switches again when he stopped. The shadows on the concrete floor had changed position. He had not noticed anything strange before, but this time he saw that the shadows were not in the same position as the last time he saw them. He noticed because two shadows that had been apart were now joined to form one large shadow. He quickly made for the light switches. Once they were on, Alan investigated the pallets of panels that caused the shadows. He looked at the floor directly behind the pallets. There were scratch marks in the concrete; the pallets had been moving. The scraping noise was caused by the movement of not one, but four or possibly five fully loaded pallets. Some force was moving the pallets across the floor, but this was only occurring when Alan was in his office. The fully loaded pallets weighed over half a ton; nothing less than a forklift truck could push the pallets across the concrete floor. There was no forklift on the upper floor area, no way of getting such a machine up there, but the pallets were being moved, slowly but surely, every time Alan returned to his office. These facts were only too apparent to Alan as he stood there, open-mouthed, looking at the scratch marks on the floor.

Could those marks have been made when the pallets were put there? he thought to himself. *Of course they could have, but the shadows on the floor were definitely different this time.*

A feeling of fear and terror was beginning to grow inside him. "Stop being so foolish," he said to himself as he tried to control the fear he felt within. A battle started in his brain, common sense fighting total and absolute terror. The battle didn't last long. Panic took over.

He ran to his office. Grabbing his coat and briefcase, he left the building as fast as his legs could carry him. He did not stop to switch off any lights or lock any doors.

The next morning the cleaners reported to me that they had found the lights on and the door unlocked when they arrived. I investigated the reasons and on my questioning Alan he apologised and told me the reasons for his behaviour. He showed me the scratch marks on the floor. They were certainly there, but whether I believed his explanation was another matter. It did seem an elaborate story just to excuse his forgetting to lock up before he went home.

During the rebuilding programme the site of the old reception area and the drawing office was used to store building materials. This site had been chosen because it was away from the new buildings and close to the roadway, providing ease in the unloading vehicles. The old building had been down for some time now, and if any supernatural events had happened in that area since then there had been no evidence of it, as the whole area was now just open land. No one spent much time there, but they still walked past to get to the other parts of the site. The smell that had been a regular event each September had not been detected since demolition, but it had not been searched for particularly. It had been forgotten about with so much activity on the site. Something did happen, however, in that area while rebuilding work was in progress. Whether it could be classified as a paranormal event is debatable, but it was strange, to say the least. . . .

Metal roof sheets, light grey in colour, had been laid on the ground almost directly on the spot the drawing office and the first-aid room had occupied. As I was project manager of the building work, the contractors would report directly to me if there were any problems or if anything occurred that needed the attention of someone in authority. This particular morning, one of the contractors came to my office. It was a cold February morning, one of those mornings that were crisp and dry. The sun was shining and the ground was hard with the overnight frost. Quite a pleasant day. We had been lucky with the weather.

"I think you had better come and have a look at this," he said after we had greeted each other with the usual morning pleasantries.

"Have we got a problem?" I asked.

"We may have, but not with the building; something must have happened on the site last night. We have not started work yet; we thought it best not to touch anything until the police have been."

"The police, what do we need the police for?" I asked. "Have we had something stolen?"

"No, nothing is missing. Come and look for yourself." He would say no more.

I followed him down the staircase and across the open land where the factory used to stand. We walked in silence. I noticed that he was not in his usual happy mood. He was a pleasant sort of chap who always had a smile on his face and a cheery word, but not this morning. I was soon to see why.

When we reached the place where the roofing sheets were stored, he stopped and pointed. He didn't need to; it was plain to see. The grey metal sheets were covered in blood, and I do mean covered. There was blood everywhere, all over the sheets, on the ground, everywhere.

"Good grief!" I exclaimed. "What has happened here?"

"It was like this when we arrived this morning. We didn't notice at first with the dark mornings, but as soon as we saw it, we stopped work and waited for you to arrive."

"I think you are right; we had better get the police," I said. "It looks to me that there has been a fight here and someone was very badly injured. I will go and phone them. In the meantime, can you and your men see if there is a trail of blood leading away? There could be someone injured and still on the site somewhere. We had better search every likely hiding place outside the factory building, but try not to disturb any evidence."

I telephoned the police and asked their advice on what to do next. They told me I had done the right thing by not disturbing anything and that they would send an officer down to investigate if a crime had been committed.

I returned to the spot where the main concentration of blood was. There was a huge amount. It is hard to describe just how much, it was spread over such a large area, but several pints at least. *What happened there during the night?* I wondered.

The contractor who had spoken to me earlier walked up to me. "There is a trail of blood leading away across the site," he said as he approached, "but it splits in two and they lead off in different directions."

I asked him to show me, and he led the way, pointing to the ground. He was pointing to blood spots that had congealed on the concrete that used to form the old factory floor. They led past the boiler house, which was still standing at the time, along what used to be the old mill, to the old flat-panel building. The trail then split into two separate trails, one leading away to the left, the other to the right. We first followed the trail to the left. It led to open land surrounded by a wire mesh fence. There was a hole in the fence, but the trail did not seem to lead towards it. The concrete finished a short way along the trail, and we lost sight of it as we came to soil and rubble left over from the demolition.

"I don't think this will lead us anywhere," I said. "Perhaps whoever it was took a wrong turn in the dark and doubled back."

We walked back to where the trail of blood separated.

The trail to the right took us out into Black Walk and under the railway bridge. It continued along the roadway for a short distance and suddenly stopped. The trail terminated with a small pool of blood that was slowly congealing. There was no evidence of blood anywhere past the pool in any direction. At that point along Black Walk, both sides of the roadway were overgrown with trees and brambles.

"Perhaps they have crawled into the undergrowth and are still there," I said. "Get some of your men and see if you can find anything. If you go onto the bridge you can look over and get a good view from up there. I'll go back and wait for the police to arrive."

As I walked back I noticed that the sun was melting the frost on the ground and some of the blood spots were disappearing as the moisture was turning the roadway black. I walked back to the contractor.

"Sorry to impose on you, but could you get someone to draw circles around the blood spots with chalk before the roadway gets too wet? Otherwise we may lose sight of them before the police get here."

He agreed to do this and I walked back to wait for the police.

It seemed a long time before the police arrived, but they did eventually arrive. Just one constable to start with, but when I showed him the amount of blood he immediately radioed for assistance and a forensic team to take blood samples. He explained that only if it was human blood could an offence have occurred. The blood could have been a result of a dogfight or something else of that nature.

"It must have been a large dog to lose that amount of blood," I said.

"It may have been several dogs," he replied. "We will know when Forensic have made a report."

When the second officer arrived they made a search of the undergrowth by the side of Black Walk, and I left them to it. They promised to keep me informed of their findings, but I never heard any more about it. it would have been nice to have an explanation for just one of the mysteries of Old Castle Works, but none was forthcoming.

This just about brings us up to the present day. Since the old factory was demolished I have built an extension to the new building and a two-storey office block and showroom on the site. I have used what influence I have to change the design and layout of the new buildings so as not to build again on the areas that had the highest concentration of sightings.

I did not say to the directors, "You cannot build there because it's haunted." I would have been laughed out of the room. No, when two or more schemes were proposed, all of equal merit, and I was asked for my recommendation, I would choose the one that had the least amount of building over areas that I knew would cause problems. I could have put forward arguments for any of them, but I chose the ones I preferred without giving my true reasons.

The site of the old reception area is now the directors' and visitors' car park, as is part of the polish shop. The other part of the polish shop has been built on and now forms part of the showroom, with the boardroom above. I thought this was very apt. If there was an appearance of a figure in there during a meeting, no one would notice. It's difficult to tell the living from the dead in there at the best of times.

The flat-panel building is still in existence, but its upper floor has been converted into a photographic studio and sublet. The boiler house also exists, but that will be the next phase of demolition and rebuilding.

There have been a few unexplainable events over the last few weeks, nothing dramatic, just little reminders that Charlie is still around. . . .

The new extension, which has been built over a year ago, is fitted with low-pressure sodium lighting. For convenience of maintenance on these lights, I had each light powered from a thirteen-amp socket, each socket fitted with a switch. This enables each light to be switched off individually and can be worked on safely without the need to turn off a whole bank of lights. Each thirteen-amp socket is fitted alongside each light in the roof, twenty-five feet from the ground.

Graham, the electrician, on one of his maintenance inspections noticed one of the lights was not working. It had been working on the previous inspections, so a sodium tube must need replacing. This particular light was right in the apex of the roof at the most inaccessible point possible. It was too high to reach by any ladders we had available, and a forklift truck fitted with a safety cage was out of the question. The floor area directly under the light was filled with benches and conveyor tracking, so a forklift truck could not get anywhere near, even if it could reach that high.

A scaffolding tower had to be leased and assembled around the benches and the tracking. Graham climbed the scaffolding only to find, when he finally reached the top, that the switch on the socket was switched off. How anyone could have reached that socket to turn off the switch I will never know, but I am used to these things by now.

I have recently received instructions to build another extension to the factory as quickly as possible. The size of this extension is to be 18,000 square feet, which means the boiler house has to come down.

I have been expecting this, so I had the smaller boiler removed and scrapped a few weeks ago. The two boilers we had shared a common chimney stack that is over nine metres high. The two boilers were connected to the stack by a one-metre-diameter ducting. This ran horizontally from the large boiler, and the small boiler joined it a few metres downstream. It then sloped up at an angle of forty-five degrees and joined the main stack. The small boiler was removed and a blanking plate fitted over the hole in the ducting that formed the chimney.

In recent days the boilerman has reported a noise within the chimney, since the other boiler was removed. He asked me to come to the boiler house and listen.

I went to the boiler house and stood directly under the stack. I waited with him, and at first I could only hear the noise of the boiler. Then I heard it, a loud rumbling noise, very loud. It ran from the boiler end along the horizontal up to the start of the forty-five degree slope and back again.

"It sounds like a cannonball running up and down," said the boilerman. It did sound just like that.

"I am not about to take the ducting down at this late stage," I said. "Just keep your eye on the ducting to watch for any sign of damage occurring. We will soon know what it is when we demolish the building."

I left it at that. He was not happy, but I was not prepared to go to all the trouble and expense of chasing noises, not when the building was coming down in a couple of weeks anyway.

I spoke to Graham of the plans to build another extension. He seemed troubled about the prospect of demolishing the boiler house. "I wonder what we will unleash when we do that," he said, trying to pass it off as a joke, but I could tell he was not really joking. Was there something about the boiler house he had not told me? Did he have an experience he did not wish to discuss? True, he had worked in the boiler house many times, in the middle of the night and sometimes alone. He had mentioned the little man in the flat cap, but what else was he keeping to himself? He was not happy at the prospect of demolition, that's for sure.

I now have to finish writing these stories. I have to concentrate on the building work. As I write these words there is a scraping noise on the other side of the wall of my office, directly behind my head. My office is on the upper floor of the new building; there is only space at the back of the wall. The workshop is twenty feet below. There are no ladders against the wall and no racking against the wall, but the scraping is there.

I know exactly what it is and exactly what is making the noise. I am not even going to bother to investigate.

I do wonder, though . . .

What is it, in the chimney?

Chapter 10

Readers, it is up to you to reach your own conclusions. If any of you have done just that, then you should read no further. If anyone who has read the stories has any strong religious beliefs, then you too, should not read any more. It is not my intention to insult or offend anyone or anyone's religious beliefs, of any denomination. To those people I thank you for reading and wish you a happy life.

For the other readers, I think I owe an explanation of sorts as to what and why these experiences of mine, and others, occur.

I would not be truthful if I said that I had not formed an opinion as to the nature of these happenings. Of course I have a theory and I have formed this theory from years of living and working with this force or forces. I would be the first to admit that there are contradictions and flaws in the theory. I do not have all the answers, but I have formulated an understanding of what happens in the factory. This helps me to live with it and changes the unknown into the familiar and so produces an acceptance, of sorts, that helps to control the fear and foreboding.

I would not attempt to put forwards a suggestion as to what the force is or where it comes from. I could easily imagine that a person with strong religious roots and upbringing who had pictures put into his head or had help with the work he was undertaking to interpret the events as divine intervention. I could just as easily imagine that a very superstitious person could interpret the contact as being in league with the Devil. My own interpretation is that both conclusions are wrong, but also both are right. Let me explain.

There is evidence to suggest that man has believed in the existence of the supernatural and spirits from as early as 10,000 B.C. There is also evidence to suggest that this belief was worldwide and existed in every culture and every civilization that we know of.

How did early man, with no previous knowledge and no one to tell him otherwise, reach these conclusions and all civilizations reach the same conclusion? Could it be that they had experiences similar to my own? Could it be that they believed in the spirit world because they knew for certain that it existed? How? Because they had experienced the power of it as I have.

As mankind developed, would it not seem possible that a certain kind of person, who had knowledge of the spirit world through his own experience, use that knowledge to promote his own position and standing in that old civilization? Could this not have given rise to the ancient religions, Greek, Roman, Egyptian, Viking, and pagan, and even witchcraft and many, many more? All these religions, which may seem primitive and crude to us, lasted many centuries. The high priest of each religion must have been able to demonstrate the existence of their own particular gods. They could not have held such influence over that many people without some sort of proof.

Could it be beyond the bounds of possibility that early man knew the locations where the force or forces made their presence felt and marked the area with stone circles and other markers? Do we really accept that ancient monuments, such as the Inca temples or the pyramids, were built by muscle power alone? For the pyramids to have been burial chambers for the great pharaohs and built for that purpose, they must all have been built in a period of one hundred years. The population of the entire world in 2500 B.C. is estimated to have been half the population of the present-day Great Britain. Where did all the manpower needed to build such great monuments, in so short a time, come from? Bearing in mind the support industries necessary for such a mammoth undertaking; ropes, rollers, scaffolding, wagons, tools, and animals. Not to mention providing food, clothes, looking after sanitary arrangements, fetching water. Who provided all those with an entire world population of only 30 million? Not forgetting that they built the great palaces and temples for the pharaohs during the same time period. Don't we think that they may just have had a little help from an energy source that we know nothing about? Yet these ancient religions died out, along with the relevant civilisations, only to be replaced by yet another civilisation with its own version of what the truth is about the spirit world. When Christianity came along it was in competition with many different forms of religion, all of which came under the heading of paganism. These pagan festivals were held in certain areas, which could possibly be the same areas that early man had discovered were special. It is highly likely that the Church found that it could not stop the local population from visiting those sites and holding their festivals. So it built its churches and monasteries at these locations. Not all the sites were built upon, but most of the main ones were. I believe that the site of Old Castle Works is just such a site.

From that time, if and when someone had a supernatural experience, providing the vision or happening was in keeping with the teachings of the Church, it was labelled a miracle. If it did not promote the teachings of the Church, it was labelled the work of the Devil. No one was allowed to have supernatural encounters unless they strongly supported and reinforced the Church's teachings. Anyone who did and from it received some sort of power or talent was labelled a witch and dealt with quickly. The Church did this from a fear that their authority would be undermined and passed it off as being for the good of the people. Up and until the birth of the electronic age, for anything to be accepted as existing it either had to be detectable by any one of our five senses or the church had to say it existed. Anything that occurred outside those parameters was classified as:

1. A sign from heaven.
2. Something that had not really happened.
3. The work of the Devil.

With the birth of the electronic age we have discovered that there exists light we cannot see, sounds we cannot hear, smells we cannot smell, forces we cannot feel. We have light that can cut through steel, sound that can be used for cleaning, microwaves that can create heat and detect movement, X rays and gamma rays that can pass through solid objects, etc., etc.

So now we have different parameters. Now a thing can only exist if it can be detected by any of our five senses or one of our electronic devices or if the Church says it exists. Anything else is:

1. A sign from heaven.
2. Something that did not really happen.
3. The work of the Devil.

We have not progressed very far, have we?

I believe there is a force that is unknown to modern-day science. It has intelligence and it is located in areas that have been clearly marked throughout history. Why it cannot move from those areas I do not know. Where it comes from I do not know. What I do know is that it is real and it is as old as the world itself. My opinion on how it communicates and why has been formulated from my own experiences. It communicates by placing pictures in the mind of whoever is responsive enough to receive them, not voices, as there is no sound or language. Its purpose seems to be to help and protect that recipient and seek acknowledgement of its own existence. If I may summarise my own experiences, I was slowly subjected to events that worried and confused me. The events built up over a period of about eighteen months and reached a climax where I was in a state of total and absolute desperation. I was then terrifed out of all description, but I got through it. Shortly after that I started to receive pictures in my mind that were so real that I am convinced I saw actual events, and my questions and problems were answered. This is how things are today: the pictures still come to me whenever I have a problem to solve. I am not saying that every answer I receive is the correct one nor that it is the one I would like to have, but it helps; it helps me a lot.

From these experiences I can only conclude that the whole thing was a sequence of events with the sole purpose of conditioning me to a mental state where I was responsive to the transmissions. From this I feel that this force can produce images for people to see, smells, noises, and feelings of cold or uneasiness. It does this in order to reduce the person to a severe state of mental confusion and produce the correct conditions within the mind of that person for contact to be made.

When the human mind is subjected to this, the strength of the individual determines whether he accepts the pictures as a reality or fights them and resists them and thus is reduced to permanent insanity. The correct conditions within the mind of the person are induced by fear, severe pain, total frustration, or complete desperation and perhaps a combination of any of those mentioned.

These energy forces will produce images that have the best desired effect: monks where a monastery used to be, white ladies or knights in armour at stately homes, victims at the scene of a crime, soldiers on a battlefield—whatever the intended recipient expects to see. These forces will move objects, switch lights on and off, and bang on walls, all for the purpose of producing absolute fear within the person's mind. This probably makes the brain produce chemicals that makes the part of the brain not normally used receptive to the transmissions. Once contact has been made, the section of the mind has been activated, it stays that way, and all is revealed; what is happening becomes as clear as day. Unfortunately, I feel that many people have suffered permanent mental disorder by this inducement, and that is regrettable.

As I have said, I have based my theory on my own experience. I accept that this is not the only possible explanation for all the events and is full of contradictions. It is, however, what happened to me, and it is my opinion that many people have experienced sightings, noises, etc., but not many have endured them. They probably left the area as fast as they could, and who can blame them for that? I had such experiences and was receptive to them. I did not leave the area, so I endured them and I was reduced to a mental state of confusion, frustration, and sheer desperation. I then started to receive pictures in a part of my brain that I was not conscious of using before.

To me this explanation is acceptable and helps me live with this force. I would *not* recommend any one subject himself to such an ordeal for the sole purpose of trying to make contact with these forces. They are in command of the situation. They are not human, so they may not have the feelings of compassion or pity we have. They, if they choose, could use their power to subject the person who dares to take charge of the situation to the most unimaginable torment. Leave well enough alone until such time as science has a better understanding of the spirit world, but remember that the human emotion of fear is their method of first starting the process towards making contact. Controlling fear is the best protection. To try to prove or disprove the existence of these forces with the use of cameras or electronic devices is as futile as trying to create nuclear power by rubbing two sticks together, and just as primative.